Copyright © 2015 by Donald Connolly
All rights reserved.

Green Ivy Publishing
1 Lincoln Centre
18W140 Butterfield Road
Suite 1500
Oakbrook Terrace IL 60181-4843

ISBN: 978-1-942901-77-8

FOREWORD TO "THE BLUE-EYED ENSIGN"

With World War II still vivid in the memory of the United States Coast Guard, the Service in the early 1950's was transitioning from war to its normal peace time duties of law enforcement, rescue at sea and maritime safety. Its officer corps was augmented by an Officer Candidate program which brought young recent college graduates into the service. The Blue-Eyed Ensign is the story of one of these newly minted officers as he goes from a college campus in Missouri to the far reaches of the Pacific Ocean. The story of how a war-hardened Coast Guard and a 'blue-eyed ensign' adjust to each other and each become the better for it, makes for a heartwarming and sometimes hilarious tale.

Woven into the story is the Ensign's love of the theater and his successful effort to bring live theater to Coast Guard and Navy men and their families on the island of Guam in the far Pacific. On the way he serves with an only slightly older officer, graduate of the US Coast Guard Academy, who was destined to become the future Commandant of the Coast Guard. Some 60 year later, the ensign (now a retired reserve Commander) and the now retired Commandant meet by chance in Washington DC and renew their friendship leading me to write this foreword. You will like this book.

Paul A. Yost, Admiral USCG (Ret)

THE BLUE-EYED ENSIGN

An Unlikely Memoir of the Korean War

by
Donald Connolly

Chapter One

Crazy? Impulsive?

There's a writing project on my desk, a small hard-cover book entitled *MY DAD. His Stories. His Words.* Each page has a heading that asks a question for Dad to answer in the blank lines that fill the page. Something for your kids to have—about your growing up, important events, attitudes, even advice.

Toward the very end, there's a question: "Dad, what's the craziest or most impulsive thing you've ever done?"

That has taken some thought. I've never considered myself impulsive. I do cherish a card for my 70th birthday: "There are those who tiptoe, and then there is you. With admiration." That's not the same as impulsive. Adventuresome, creative maybe, that's what that is, isn't it?

The answer that finally occurred to me was at least partly crazy at the time and certainly more than a bit impulsive: a college graduate with an English major, from the middle of the country, with no boating experience, applying for Officer Candidate School in the U.S. Coast Guard during the Korean War.

The war started in June 1950, and when I graduated from college in 1952, the war looked far from ending and any healthy male my age was eligible to be drafted into the army.

The Draft, as conscription into the military is called in the United States, was enacted by Congress in 1940, the first peacetime involuntary call-up in history, during the early days of World War II in Europe. It was implemented until 1973 when all military service became voluntary; it is still in place today as a contingency plan. There have been several versions in that time, tweaked to satisfy the prevailing requirements. For example, in 1948 the Selective Service Act included the "Doctor Draft," wherein health professionals could be called up for 21 months of active duty and 5 years of reserve affiliation.

In 1952 I was under the 1951 Universal Military Training and Service Act which required two years of service from men 18½ to 26 years of age, who were healthy and had no deferments, such as schooling or parenthood. As of September 1952, neither of those deferments, or any other, applied to me.

Military service was not a major consideration when I started college in 1948; there was no active war and only a few thousand men were being drafted each year. My full scholarship at St. Louis University depended on good academic performance, so joining the school's Air Force ROTC never entered my mind. Two of my brothers had been in the army in World War II, had survived and were pursuing studies and careers. When the Korean War started, I shrugged and said, I'll worry about that when I get finished with this.

Deep down, I didn't want to be involved, and even though by graduation time it was clear I would be, other things were happening.

My brother Gene, eight years older, was to be ordained a priest in the Passionist order in Louisville, Kentucky, something very special for the whole family. About the time of my graduation, he would celebrate his first solemn Mass in our parish church in Normandy, Missouri, a suburb of St. Louis. A reception would follow in the parish hall, but there would be visitors to our house, and the sprucing up – stair treads and kitchen floor tiles replaced, woodwork painted, etc. – fell on me.

The ordination, first Mass and reception came and went, as did the month of July.

In August, the notice arrived for my army physical; it was scheduled in early September, a prospect that can sharpen your interest in performing your military service elsewhere, if you can.

Out of the blue, it turned out that might be possible.

The enabler was Bob McCormick, a former professor in the drama department at St. Louis University, who was serving his two-week reserve training duty at the Coast Guard District office in St. Louis the first two weeks in September.

"You're waiting to be drafted?!"

Some of his students had gathered for a Saturday night reunion with him.

"What for?" he continued. "You want to be an officer!"

"What are you talking about?"

"You can, in the Coast Guard."

"I don't know anything about boats!"

"That doesn't matter. Come down Monday and we'll get you started."

I'm from St. Louis. On the Mississippi River, yes, but almost as far from ocean-type bodies of water as you can get. I could swim—swimming was a favorite activity as a kid – but I knew nothing about boats, or ships, or the difference between them. Only once had I even seen the ocean, the year before, in Oregon. And the Coast Guard was a mystery to me. It was a surprise to learn that the service was responsible for navigable waterways in the interior of the country, like the Mississippi and Ohio rivers, and the headquarters for that activity, the Second District, was in downtown St. Louis.

My oldest brother, Jim, still at home, had been in the Army Air Corps in World War II. "Kid," he said ominously, "the Coast Guard doesn't want English majors, they want engineers."

Who else to turn to? My father died when I was ten years old. The two brothers between Jim and me weren't available – Gene was a new priest, Bob was married and finishing his studies to be a chiropractor. Jim was very smart, but then, my future was at stake and I was willing to try anything.

Early that Monday morning, Mac greeted me at the Second Coast Guard District Headquarters in downtown St. Louis and led me to the personnel office. They gave me a bunch of forms to fill out and instructions about transcripts and letters of recommendation and police records. By Friday, I had everything needed and returned them all to the Coast Guard personnel office.

They knew of my pending induction physical and were willing to expedite the other requirements: an interview with three senior Coast Guard officers and a preliminary physical. Both were scheduled for early the next week.

The interviewing officers were friendly and polite, fatherly, even grandfatherly. They were lined up on one side of the table; I sat across – alone. They asked about my background, education, sailing experience, and other things I don't remember. But eventually – and I do remember this – they asked why

I wanted to join the Coast Guard. No doubt it was a rambling response, and no doubt they were wondering how I would get around not saying I wanted to avoid the draft. It was easy, and honest, to say I liked that the Coast Guard was a small organization, that its mission was not just military but had a lot of peacetime functions, serving civilian shipping and waterways, running lighthouses, rescuing flood victims, things like that.

There was no way to judge what they were thinking. A glance at my university transcript showed two math courses, but it was heavy with philosophy, Latin and Greek, and literature and theatre. The letters of recommendation were from adults who liked me, so they would be positive and likely exaggerated.

As kindly and respectful as the officers were, they didn't tip their hand.

The preliminary physical was the usual stuff – eyes, heart, lungs, feet, height and weight – to be sure there were no disqualifying conditions. The hospital corpsman on duty was a fellow I recognized from high school and college, a year older and a year ahead of me. Tom had gone to Officer Candidate School after graduation but had flunked out. He went to corpsman school and was serving his required military time as a Hospital Corpsman 3rd Class at the infirmary at the St. Louis office, giving preliminary physicals and assisting the Public Health Service medical doctor assigned there.

It was a comfort to learn about Officer Candidate School from someone who had recently been there, but the flunking concerned me. Would I have the same problem? He wasn't bitter; he said he had enjoyed the school but he just couldn't do what was expected.

My health was good and Tom found no problems, until I stepped on the scale. Weight 165 pounds. Height 5 feet 8 inches. Doesn't seem bad, but the insurance company guide book Tom had to follow listed the normal weight as 154 pounds.

I had been lifting weights since my brother Jim came home from World War II and bought some barbells and dumbbells. My interest in the weights was in response to my ever-present feeling of being overweight, as I had been as a kid. Twelve years old, 5 feet tall, 175 pounds. You grow taller and stretch that fat out, so to speak, but if you want to play sports or look good for the girls, you have to have some muscles. I didn't have a lot of muscles, but the curling, squatting and pressing had given me enough bulk to move the scales beyond "normal."

"I'm going to put down 154," Tom said. "We don't want to raise a red flag that would give them some little thing to reject you."

I said, "Thanks." But my optimism was waning: maybe this was a crazy idea? — honestly, had I been too impulsive?

The next week I took my Army physical. There were no problems mentioned so apparently I passed. Now it was the waiting game.

A friend down the street, Jerry Dwyer, took the physical with me. We both attended St. Ann's Church and would see each other most Sundays after the 11 o'clock Mass. No, he hadn't heard anything from the draft board; neither had I. It went on this way for a month, until mid-October.

"Did you hear anything?"

"Yeah – last week. Didn't you?"

He was scheduled to report for induction in a few weeks. Maybe my notice was delayed in the mail, maybe it would show up in a day or so. It didn't. About a week later a letter from the Coast Guard arrived. I had been accepted. The letter instructed me to report to the Reserve Training Center located at the Coast Guard Academy in New London, Connecticut, on November 25th – depending upon two things:

My draft board had to be informed immediately to be sure it was okay with them.

And there would be another physical, this time by the Coast Guard doctor, before my departure.

The draft board serving our area was in Ferguson, about 5 miles beyond our community of Normandy. It was late afternoon and Jim had the car at work. "Immediately" is an intimidating word. I hurried, letter in hand, to the bus stop a block away, hopped on the next bus, and prayed the draft board office would be open.

The small office of four or five people was quietly active. I presented the letter to the receptionist who directed me to the woman at the desk behind her. She scanned the letter quickly and nodded her head. "Connolly – " she said to herself, and reached to the file box on the tall cabinet beside her, took down the folder on top and opened it. She didn't have to look for the name.

"Okay," she said "The Coast Guard told us you had applied. We held up your notice 'til we heard from them." She took the copy and put it in my folder, put the folder in another file box and gave my letter back to me. "If you don't go in, you make sure you let us know. Understand?" No 'congratulations,' no 'good luck.'

"Yes, ma'am."

On the bus back I re-read the letter at least four or five times. New London, Connecticut – I had never been in the eastern part of the country. November – it will probably be cold, but St. Louis gets cold, too. Going there by train – that would be okay, I had done a lot of train travel, my father having been an accountant for the Wabash Railroad.   Officer Candidate School – OCS – what would that really be like? Would everybody else know all about ships and nautical stuff? Would they all be engineers? Was I going to be in over my head?

I had four weeks to think about that. If the phony weight on my preliminary physical didn't get me rejected.

After the first physical I had tried to lose weight. In college I drank little beer or booze of any kind, and didn't now and didn't gorge on anything at home or away. I tried to cut back on bread and sweets. But Mom and Gram were cooking, and most of my time was spent just waiting around. I even tried steam baths – actually sauna-type plaitzes where you get really heated up, wetted down and scrubbed with a soft brush. But the scale didn't change.

The official physical was going well. HM3 Tom was there, assisting the doctor, taking down the numbers. The doctor was pleasant but serious, not impressed with the normal readings and attributes of a normal 22-year old male. Tom kept the preliminary folder out of the way, as much as he could.

I stepped on the scale. 165 pounds. For some reason this time the doctor reached for folder.

"Last time you were 154?"

My heart sank.

He showed the page to Tom who studied it seriously. To me he said, "You gained 11 pounds in 6 weeks?" I looked at Tom and then at him.

"No, sir – I'm sure I didn't – my clothes still fit the same."

To Tom he said, "What do you think happened?"

Tom shook his head. "I don't know. Maybe the scale got stuck last time." Whether he had rehearsed that or made it up on the spur of the moment, it sounded pretty good to me.

The doctor studied the numbers, then my waist line.

"Well, you don't have any rolls hanging over your shorts. You're okay. You pass."

He signed the exam. Tom nodded. I exhaled.

Chapter Two

Recalling

What prompts me to tell about events that happened so long ago? That "Dad" book played a part, once again. A couple of questions led me to dig through some stuff on shelves in our second bedroom where my desk is. Barbara and I moved to this apartment eleven years ago, downsizing from a comfortable 80-year-old three-bedroom home we had lived in for 25 years. In the years here we've gone through several cycles of tossing stuff, and in the process other stuff has surfaced, especially papers and photos we want to keep.

During one clean-out I found an expandable brick-colored folder with a large brown envelop inside marked "Coast Guard." Clipped together were typed pages whose small Elite font revealed they had been written with the Hermes typewriter I bought in Hawaii in 1953. I had put part of those papers into a three-ring binder and eventually consolidated them all into a special folder with pockets on each side.

In one pocket was a journal started during my service in the Coast Guard.

In the other pocket were letters I wrote home from my duty stations. My mother saved them. I asked her to, but she had already started doing so. Maybe it's the kind of thing mothers do. Barbara recently showed me letters and cards our kids wrote to us. She also saved some early letters and cards from me; some heavy breathing there – or does it just seem that way now?

My plan is to incorporate that journal and my letters into this story, fleshing them out with my own memories. I'm 83 years old, but my memory is good and my time as a Blue-Eyed Ensign, and the events leading up to it, were rich and rewarding, and therefore memorable. Also at hand is a good scrapbook, photos (black and white, maybe some Polaroid), programs, and memorabilia, to jog the memory cells.

Some of the conversations reported here I remember as if

a tape was running in my brain; others will approximate what was said. Some names may be altered to avoid possible but needless embarrassment.

So I will put my current thoughts and recollections about the years ago into the mix with the journal and the letters, and do my best to be accurate and to make it enjoyable for you.

Chapter Three

OCS

Late November 1952, two days before Thanksgiving, I reported to Coast Guard Officer Candidate School in New London, Connecticut. It was my first time east of Detroit. The train journey was uneventful, but to my mind the East seemed a bit different, kind of foreign. The people in Philadelphia and New York spoke with accents I had only heard in the movies. Looking out the train windows and waiting at stations to change trains, I saw crowded and dirty places, without trees or softening colors. It was late November, and no doubt that affected the images – gray dominated nature's palate.

The parent facility for the OC School was the Coast Guard Academy where, like the Naval Academy in Annapolis, Maryland, cadets go through four years of university-type schooling that incorporates the kinds of courses needed to be an effective officer. It is still active and thriving.

The physical presence of the OCS consisted of 3 or 4 one- or two-story buildings – a barracks, mess hall, class rooms, and offices – on the same grounds as the Academy. We were a tight square of dark frame temporary-looking World War II structures dropped onto the lovely landscaped setting of stone and brick heritage-laden edifices of three- or four-stories with winding roadways and paths linking them.

Officially and actually, there was no interaction between the two schools, except that some instructors taught in both places. You could easily tell the students apart – cadets wore double-breasted uniforms with gold buttons, with a white shirt and black tie, like all officers, except their cadet rank was on their sleeves. Officer Candidates –OCs – wore "sailor suits."

[In 1962 when Barbara and I moved into our first house, our neighbor was an active duty regular Coast Guard officer who was attending the four-year Academy when I was in the four-month OCS. In conversations I would sometimes say, "When I was at the Academy, etc. etc." – it tended to bother him.]

My class was designated 2-53: we would be the second class that would graduate in 1953, approximately 4 months after being sworn in. There were two other classes in the school, 1-53, and the last class of '52. Each class lived on its own floor in the barracks, and at first we didn't see much of the others. Like freshman at any school, we held upper-classmen somewhat in awe, wondering if they had felt like we did now, if they had picked up any special savvy that we would need, and hoping they might give us some advice.

There were thirty of us in Class 2-53, a bit smaller than the others when they started. About twenty were brand new college graduates. The others were enlisted men who had been recommended by their officers. They were older, in the upper enlisted grades—first-class or chief petty officers. We college kids were given the grade of Seaman Apprentice. We wore enlisted uniforms like the others, with two small slanted stripes on the upper left sleeve, and above that, at the shoulder seam, the letters "OC" on a patch about an inch-and-a-half square.

A raw recruit in basic training is a Seaman Recruit and wears one slanted stripe. We were one stripe above.

Seaman Apprentice (OC)
Donald A. Connolly, Class 2-53

For us college kids the academics were a continuation of what we had just experienced for four years. Our problem areas would be the practical stuff like handling boats and performing military duties such as being Junior Officer of the Day. For our enlisted classmates it was the opposite. Each group was able and eager to support the other when needed. We were in this thing together.

"Marching to class – or anywhere you go."

Then there was "adaptability" where each of us was on his own. "Adaptability" was the almost indefinable quality manifested by how you handled yourself, what kind of leadership you exhibited, your maturity and confidence, your ability to handle the pressure that developed. Plus other things – quite subjective to the evaluators – summarized in the term "gut feeling."

It was like any school, except that we marched everywhere. In the morning we assembled on the roadway between the barracks and the mess hall for roll call, then filed row by row inside for breakfast. After breakfast, we returned to our rooms, gathered our books, and re-assembled on the roadway and marched to our first class. At noon we marched back to the barracks, assembled for lunch, and marched inside. If we went to the Thames River (which forms the east boundary of the Academy) for seamanship practice in pulling boats, we marched. And if we went to the field house to learn how to march, we marched.

The marching didn't cause me any concern. I was a Boy Scout, joining in 1942 and active until I earned my Eagle rank in 1946 or 1947, and we did a lot of marching and close-order drill –"column left" "column right" "to the rear march," etc., plus the standing-still moves, "dress right—dress" "left face" "about face" "hand salute" and such.

But never had I experienced an instructor – a Drill Master – like Lieutenant Commander Melville K. Short.

Mr. Short was indeed short and on the stocky side. He was Canadian by birth, a former college instructor, we were told, with clipped, somewhat affected speech. At OCS, he taught navigation in the classroom and close-order drill in the field house, and treated both subjects as if they were the most important things you would ever need to know.

His style of teaching was both intimidating and amusing. He had a theatrical flair, using gestures, facial expressions, and precise enunciation. As much as he loved to teach, it was obvious he loved the military as well: his posture was almost rigidly erect whether standing in the classroom or striding on the tarmac; his cap was always perfectly aligned, his tailored double-breasted jacket was worn snug across his just-bulging belly where without realizing it he continually ran his fingers up and down to be sure the buttons were in fact buttoned.

Our first encounter with Mr. Short was in the field house, where all three classes were assembled. Without any instruction to us newcomers, he set our three groups in motion, the oldest class in the lead. It was only a few minutes until some in our group made wrong turns or couldn't keep the cadence and put us in disarray. Mr. Short called for all to halt and put us "at ease." The other classes were smiling. They had been through this themselves and it was their turn to enjoy our embarrassment.

Mr. Short stepped slowly and wearily to the front of our class, shaking his head. He studied our faces and let his shoulders slump. With a deep sigh, he pulled himself up straight and scanned the group.

"The Cream," he proclaimed in his clipped, rich voice, "the Cream of the Intellectual Youth of America."

The other classes couldn't keep from an audible giggle which he allowed and let die.

He continued: "If you had the intelligence that God in his infinite wisdom gave to little green apples – " Again his head shook, and he turned to the other classes and admonished them not to laugh at us, that they had been as bad and look how well they performed now.

Eventually we got instructions about military matters – assembling, moving in formation, saluting, and inspections. These were important because messing up on them was a major source of demerits, and demerits not only didn't look good on your record, they kept you from getting evening liberty into

New London for a seafood dinner or a weekend pass to go to New York or Boston. You would be in formation staring straight ahead and hear a voice on your right and turn your head a fraction – if seen by an officer, that was a demerit. Shoes not properly shined – demerits. Late from liberty – demerits.

In navigation class Mr. Short used his deliberate vocal control to explain, emphasize, correct, cajole, entice – any device that would help us understand a problem and keep the Coast Guard Cutter (CGC) Neversail and the CGC Neversink afloat and off the rocks and shoals, so you didn't hear "that familiar crunching sound." Those were the names he used for the ships in our navigation studies – obvious but appreciated humor.

Other indoor classes included gunnery, military justice, seamanship (the academic part), and anti-submarine warfare – each to be learned by studying the book and memorizing as much as we could, so we could pass the test. Some guys had a knack for a subject, or by accident did well and became an expert in the eyes of the others.

My specialty became gunnery. Within two weeks of classes we had a test and my grade was 98 or something very high. It was all memory about the .45 caliber pistol. I had never fired one, never seen one until the class. We learned to dismantle and reassemble the weapon. The explanation in the book was pretty clear, and probably appealed to the mechanical side of my brain. When the scores were posted I heard, "Wow, Connolly really knows gunnery." From then on, when there was a gunnery test, I was a consultant to the class. That meant I had to study especially hard to hold up my undeserved reputation.

In our spare time, and we did have a reasonable amount, guys would sit around and have bull sessions, write letters, listen to music, and read. My roommate, John Davey was a jazz fan with his own record player. He especially liked the New York City night club singer Lee Wiley; he had her records and played them all the time. When I could get him to take a break, we listened to original cast records of Broadway shows. Especially popular was "New Faces of 1952," provided by one of the guys and enjoyed by most everyone.

My reading at the time was *The Caine Mutiny* and I was

stunned by the beginning about Willie Keith in Navy OCS in New Haven, the way he passed the physical and how he became an expert, and the way he passed some of the classes. It was all happening again in New London.

Christmas was approaching and we began to wonder how the school would treat the holidays. Regular classes or time off? Certainly the instructors and office personnel didn't want to hang around at Christmas. But this was the military and days away had to be counted as leave, and we hadn't earned any leave. And maybe some of our guys wouldn't want to be away; maybe they had no place to go.

So we learned about "basket leave."

Yes, we would all be allowed to be away, "on leave," from before Christmas until after New Year's Day, about a week and a half. We'd have to find our own transportation to wherever we wanted to go, which for most of us was home. Leave papers were cut for each one of us; we signed them, got a copy, and the originals were put in a basket on the chief yeoman's desk. When we returned in early January all copies would be destroyed; we were never away. As I recall, some guys were allowed to stay on the base.

In a "small world" moment, a fellow in Class 1-53 had attended Washington University in St. Louis and performed in their 1952 musical for which I wrote the lyrics. He lived in Belleville, Illinois, near St. Louis, and had a car in New London. So just before Christmas, Lee Harrison drove me and several others to points along the Pennsylvania Turnpike and US Highway 40 between Philadelphia and St. Louis. It was a long drive, mostly in the dark, with no major stops. The car was jammed with people and baggage and the Turnpike provided the only express highway on the route. But it was worth any discomfort to have the unexpected time away after only four weeks in school, and to be with family and friends for the holidays.

Meals with family and the usual visits to friends' homes meant that food and drink were abundant and ever-present. A kind of euphoria had taken hold of me – I was doing okay in the military and could tell stories about a new and different life –

and I felt no concern about what I ate. When the time came to get to Belleville for the ride back to New London, I had gained almost ten pounds. Once again my nemesis of weight-gain had beaten me.

Tom Alberger had the same problem. He was one of the enlisted men in the class, in his late twenties, a first-class petty officer with about eight years under his belt. He could also put a good amount of Budweiser beer under his belt. He couldn't afford to go home on leave, but went to New York or Boston and stayed in some military lodging or a YMCA. A gregarious guy, he loved to socialize, talk and drink, and no doubt he had found entertainment and companionship. I remember his affinity for Budweiser because he complained about the brewer, Anheuser-Busch, starting to brew the beer in multiple cities around the country, not just in St. Louis.

"It's not the same water," he complained. "That's part of the taste."

Tom and I both knew we needed motivation if we were going to lose weight. We found a scale, weighed ourselves, wrote the numbers down and put that and ten dollars each into an envelope. At graduation, or dismissal, which was an overhanging prospect, whoever had lost the most weight would get the money. The money was mostly symbolic; the connection with Tom and the friendly competition gave us a little diversion as well as motivation when we needed it.

After the holiday leave we settled into school quite seriously. The senior class had graduated before Christmas, and a new class was scheduled to arrive in a few weeks. We were moving up, getting deeper into the subjects, and approaching the time when we would have responsibility for musters, marching, and running the military side of our barracks. We would be Junior Officer of the Day, JOOD, under a senior officer's supervision, of course; they weren't going to let us make a mess of everything.

The deep of winter in Connecticut, on the Thames River, close to Block Island Sound and the Atlantic Ocean, can be cold. That year it was, especially the wind chill. When we marched to class, our peacoats were usually buttoned high at the neck, every one of them, as instructed at muster by the JOOD, to ensure all uniforms were, in fact, uniform.

Besides the usual discomfort, the cold and wind teamed up to deliver a potential blow to success at OCS, definitely to mine.

Our practical training in seamanship took place on the Thames River. There was a boat house and dock that accommodated a small number of wooden pulling boats – the kind propelled by pulling on oars – of the type called a "monomoy."

Several times a week our class would fill two or three boats, each with eight or ten rowers and one coxswain. Many of us had to learn how to row properly, how to "feather the blade" with our wrists at the proper time to get the most pull and least resistance, how and when to put the oars vertical in boat when docking or passing an obstacle, how to keep from "catching a crab" by letting your oar get out of control. Not that we would ever have duty as oarsmen or coxswains. But it was a basic foundation for being a Man of the Sea.

The oarsmen sat two abreast on thwarts ("tharts"), hard wooden seats that spanned the boat; the coxswain stood at the stern facing the rowers, calling commands to control the course and speed, to launch and dock the craft, and most importantly, to keep the rowers in rhythm by calling "pull" "pull" " pull". We took turns being the coxswain, moving from thwart to thwart in rotation. It was great exercise, and as I began to lose weight, for the first time (and maybe the last) I saw some abdominal muscles – a fledgling six-pack at best, but mine.

You soon realized that you were learning to work as a team. Your success as a coxswain was very much in the hands of your oarsmen who had to give that extra effort when needed to counter the wind or get past an obstacle, or to respond rapidly to an "oars" command. And they relied on you to get them where they were supposed to go and to keep them safe; they were rowing backwards.

When there was a wind on the river, the splashes from the oars were blown into the boat and froze instantly, not only on the metal oarlocks which held the oars in place, but also on the wooden thwarts. I couldn't help but develop a little parody on John Greenleaf Whittier:

> "When the ice is on the oarlock,
> And also on the thwart,
> Be careful when you rotate,
> Or you'll tear you ass apart."

It was late February when we marched to the river for our only graded test in Practical Seamanship.

Even in gloves, our hands were cold. Even in our fatigues, or work clothes, with extra sweaters, socks and underwear, our bodies shivered from the moment we got to the boat house. At least mine did. We pushed the boats away from the docks, the first coxswain at his post and in control, and headed for a section of the river where an obstacle course had been set up – two or three pairs of oars stuck into the river bottom, each pair about ten feet apart. Just getting to the test course required maneuvers against the wind which was easily pushing the boat off course.

I don't recall if we got any practice runs; we probably did. What I remember is the actual run that would account for a big part of our grade in seamanship. Our evaluator, sitting in the bow, was a Chief Warrant Officer, newly assigned to the school. We had never seen him before, nor he us. He knew what we were supposed to do, and would grade us accordingly.

By the time my turn as coxswain came, all of us were aware of the sideways push of the wind and realized we would have to be extra careful and extra helpful to each other, if we could. I took the boat to the starting point near the middle of the river and gave the commands that headed us toward the first obstacle. The wind was gusty, unpredictable. I can't recall exactly what happened; I either made one obstacle and missed the other two, or made two and missed one. I do remember feeling helpless as we approached one obstacle as fast as we could and calling "oars!" which had the rowers raise their oars vertically to avoid the embedded obstacle oars, only to feel the wind push the boat to the side and totally miss the target.

I also remember looking at the evaluator and saying, "Should I try again?" and he just shaking his head and writing on his pad.

A day or two later when the grades were posted on the bulletin board (for all to see), I stared at the grade sheet wondering if it was possible to flunk seamanship and still get a commission. My grade was 33%.

That seemed pretty severe to me, and I asked the evaluator how he came to that number. His explanation was a confusing mix of what I had done and what I hadn't done. But there was no changing it.

Maybe this whole Coast Guard thing was *more* than a bit impulsive – maybe it was *totally crazy*!

We were now about six weeks from graduation. Many guys had left the class, some of the college kids, some of the enlisted men. My friend Alberger was gone; it was just too much work for him. He won the weight-loss contest, but it was a pleasure to pay the ten dollars to be as thin as I had been in a long time, about 155 pounds.

The days went on and no "call to the office" came about seamanship. However, my fingers remained crossed.

It was common to feel and to talk about the pressure we were under. So we looked for any way to get out from under. A special escape was a weekend in New York City – leaving Friday night or Saturday morning and returning Sunday night – a short train-ride away. I went several times to see Broadway shows and visit friends from St. Louis University, all of whom were trying to break into show business. Another escape was in the field house where pick-up basketball games were always available on weekends. I wasn't a very good athlete – coordinated but not experienced because my extra weight caused me to shy away from organized sports at school – the last kid picked for a team in physical education class was me. Swimming was fine, even in my shape, because that wouldn't mess up anybody's game. Fortunately, nobody took the basketball seriously so I managed to participate, work the muscles, and forget about studies.

I also managed to sprain my ankle.

One of the players was Galen Nielsen, a chief engineman

from the west coast in class 3-53 who had played a lot of sports and recognized immediately that I needed medical attention. He helped me get to the infirmary where they put tape on my ankle and a white armband with a red cross on my coat sleeve. The arm band declared to all around that the wearer was injured and exempt from obligations such as formations and marching.

From then until I was declared healed, whenever the platoon mustered and headed in formation to the class room, I stood separately, at 'attention' as best I could, and then followed along behind at my own pace, at first with a crutch. This had happened about midway in the training, and it was a relief to avoid some of the military stress points. But payback came – the first day off of the sick list and back in formation, I got demerits for unmilitary bearing at muster.

Apparently what counted most in the military-bearing category was how you performed as Junior Officer of the Day. And it was truly a performance, in the sense that we were doing something we'd never done before, something not in our usual range of activity, and needing continuous focus on the role. There was even a "costume" that set you apart: we wore khaki leggings with pants tucked in at the shins, a web belt at our waist (over the peacoat if we were outdoors), and an armband with capital letters "JOOD." There was no missing what your job was.

The JOOD activities took place mostly in the office at the ground-floor entrance to the barracks and in the muster area in the roadway. The assignment lasted one full day, from morning till night. Duties consisted of handling the schedules and announcements for all three classes, answering the phone and taking messages, calling muster and taking roll call and turning the platoons over to their leaders to march them to classes. A lot of it was common sense – you were part secretary, part gate-keeper, part guide and part instructor. The Senior Officer wasn't with you the whole time – he had a class or other duties and showed up at musters so you could make your reports to him and he could join you in the mess hall for meals. And there you had to make extended conversation with him.

Our class was down to twenty members by the time it

was our turn to take over the JOOD duties. It was possible we would have the assignment more than once. My first assignment is a blur, but my second is fixed in my memory because it was with Mr. Short.

I had come to appreciate and like Mr. Short. He cared about us. In navigation class he gave extra attention to anyone having difficulty. In the final weeks of the program, when we were dealing with celestial navigation, he announced he would come back after the evening meal and give us instructions about the constellations and planets as we could see them in the winter sky. Our attendance was voluntary, of course, but, of course, no one missed it.

He made the star-gazing enjoyable and informative. I had earned an astronomy merit badge in the Boy Scouts and was able to ask reasonable questions and respond to his.

A few days later it was my turn to serve under him as JOOD.

For the evening meal we mustered as usual in the roadway in front of the mess hall. By this time the process of mustering the troops, taking reports from squad leaders, doing an about-face, and reporting to the SOOD had become routine. The saluting was now automatic. I was very comfortable.

Darkness came in late afternoon and the winter sky that particular evening was clear and ablaze with some of the constellations we had been studying.

As the men filed into the mess hall, I stood with Mr. Short.
"Beautiful night, sir, isn't it?"
"Yes, it is."
I looked up.
"You sure can see Orion tonight." The winter constellation was high and seemed to dominate the sky. The belt of three stars and the sword of three more, with bright stars at the head and feet made it easy to identify.

Mr. Short and I followed the men inside and went to our separate table. Everyone was standing at attention beside their chairs. "Seats," I called. We all sat and a soft conversational buzz arose as we waited for the food to be served.

How do I start the conversation with Mr. Short? Do I

dare - - ?

"You know, Mr. Short—" He looked at me.

"You know, I understand that Orion means there's at least one Irishman in heaven."

His eyes stayed glued to my face. He didn't speak, he just kept looking, until a frown evolved into a quizzical expression.

"I'm afraid I don't understand. Orion – Orion is a figure in Greek mythology –"

His voice trailed off. I sighed and swallowed.

In the barest whisper, I muttered, "O'Ryan, Mr. Short. O'Ryan."

His frown remained for a moment, then gave way to a feeble smile.

"Oh, I see."

No doubt we spoke of other things as we ate, but all I could think about was the weak joke that had totally missed its mark.

The weeks were passing and we all put in extra time preparing for final exams. It was then that The Poop appeared. There were rumors that copies of exams resided in the upper classes and somehow they would be handed down to us. Not that those tests were always repeated, we were told; you couldn't count on anything like getting the exact exam, word for word. The Poop would give you a good idea of what to study, and maybe you would learn something from the question-answer proximity on the test form.

My grades in the academics were good, about average. The class had our extremes on both ends. Ty Allen seemed to be a nautical natural and was acing just about every subject, including Practical Seamanship. His college friend and roommate, Bob Albert, had already been dismissed. They were the original "odd couple": Ty was short and wiry, Bob was a big football player, heavily muscled; Ty was disciplined and studious, Bob was easily side-tracked – looking up a definition in the dictionary, he would read the other words on the page because he found them fascinating.

Grade-wise, I was somewhere in the middle and happy

to be there.

Except for Seamanship. You couldn't get any lower than I was – that 33% from the pulling boat fiasco would be figured in with my grades on the academic side of the course. How was it possible to get a passing grade for the whole subject when you start out with a 33? And if I didn't pass, what would that mean? My jazz-loving roommate, John Davey, couldn't march; try as he might, he could not keep cadence. He was still there.

We knew the expectations, the standards. What were the variables?

The Poop arrived, covering most of the subjects. I looked at all of them, but held onto the seamanship exams as long as possible, scouring and practically memorizing them. Memorizing came easy, necessary for learning lines for plays in high school and college; with that came a visual awareness that put words and numbers on paper in relationships that my brain found easy to recall. Not a photographic memory, but a recall based on visual association. It is still pretty strong.

Along with the final exams, we got into bits and pieces of preparations for being commissioned – if in fact we would be.

Evaluations were still going on to determine our "adaptability." Hank Middleton was called to the office to discuss something he had checked on our entrance application, declaring he was a "conscientious libertine." Not many of us knew what that meant; maybe he didn't, either. He was fairly "liberal" in his outlook, as I recall; maybe that's what he meant. The word "libertine" sounded old-fashioned to me, out of the "roaring twenties." Hank came back from the interview a bit chagrined, but still in the school. He never explained what happened.

New uniforms had to be acquired – officer uniforms! Tailors from a local uniform shop showed up and took our measurements. And pictures had to be taken, in an officer uniform, including a "hard hat" – portraits to be sent to our local newspapers announcing our commissioning. We had no say in either activity. Not that we wanted anything more than to get the appropriate clothing, get appropriate pictures taken, get our orders (a big item, of course) and leave OCS behind us as an officer in the United States Coast Guard Reserve.

That outcome, we felt, could still be affected by how we did on our final exams.

The exams were scheduled with reasonable spacing between them. There were eighteen of us left in the class and everyone seemed reasonably confident. Only fear of the unknown bothered us. Everyone knew about my seamanship situation and avoided talking about it.

There were few surprises in any of the exams. Especially and happily for me, there was no surprise at all in the seamanship exam. When the instructor gave the okay and I flipped the exam paper over to start the test, very familiar words lay before me. It was one of the Poop exams, word for word.

Slowly and carefully I went through each question, multiple-choice, marking off each answer with confidence, almost excitement. I took my time because I didn't want to suggest that I was just remembering, not thinking. It was a pleasant experience.

The grades were posted. Mine was 97, maybe 100. I don't recall exactly, but it was almost perfect. For the whole course, with the 33 cranked in, my grade was 71. That number I remember. I had passed seamanship. I would graduate.

The commissioning would be a separate ceremony from the graduation, occurring on Thursday, April 2, followed by a dinner with our instructors who would then be our "fellow officers." The graduation would be the next day.

Graduating OCs assembling to go to Commissioning ceremony.

A few days before those events, our officer uniforms arrived. We put them on and turned in our sailor suits. It was strange, almost bizarre, to be in officer uniforms, in white shirts with black ties, to look at one another and see a different image of a guy who had shared studies and struggles for four months, sometimes in dungarees, sometimes in Dress Blues, now wearing hard hats and sporting a single shiny gold stripe near the end of his sleeves. The caps with the hard beaks were heavy compared to the cloth ones we had worn. They didn't sit well on everyone; they took breaking in and getting used to.

We were in a kind of a limbo, hanging around and gabbing, packing and making travel arrangements, doing any paper work needed.

Finally, with much excitement, we learned our assignments: Mine was contained in Order No. 512021, dated 25 March 1953, from Commandant to Superintendent, U. S. Coast Guard ACADEMY, New London, Conn.:

> "Effective upon execution of oath of office and when released by the Superintendent, CG ACADEMY, the following personnel are hereby detached from all duties previously assigned. The personnel involved are hereby called to extended active duty and will proceed and report to the Commander, Western Area, San Francisco, Calif., for assignment to indoctrination in controller duties."

Then, under the heading: <u>NAME</u> (All Reserve Ensigns): "Merrill L. DUBACH, Jr. and Donald A. CONNOLLY"

Dated March 25th? You mean – I had been considered an Ensign a week earlier, and didn't have to sweat anything!? Even the seamanship exam? Was that possible – ?

But – wait – this is now and – what in heaven's name are "controller duties"? I had never heard that phrase before; that kind of duty had never been mentioned in any of our training. It means working in a Rescue Coordination Center, I was told, which didn't clarify anything, except – Not on a ship? Well, maybe that was just as well with my seamanship record. In San Francisco?! Wow! Not necessarily, I was told, probably somewhere in the Pacific.

Like the new uniforms, the commissioning ceremony at first seemed unreal. Faces you had responded to solemnly in a military and academic context were smiling and congratulating you and being friendly. When talking to them, you still used their military titles. You realized you didn't know their first names.

A couple of enlisted men were as pleased as we were about our commissioning. They waited at the door and saluted each of us as we left the room. It was our first salute as an officer, and according to custom, each of us had to pay them a dollar.

I had used the waiting time to write a poem about the class, the people and their memorable traits. The thread of the poem had to be special. No problem there – it would be something we had learned from Mr. Short. I read it at the dinner.

> "While assembling my belongings the other day, I chanced to thumb through my seamanship book, and this sheet of paper fell to the floor. It turned out to be something I had penned in an unconscious state resulting from an overdose of Navpers Instruction books. It is respectfully dedicated to all future OC's, and is blasphemously entitled, 'The Sinking of the Neversink.'
>
> > You've heard her called the Neversink,
> > Well, gentlemen, that's bunk,
> > For let this serve to tell you
> > The Neversink has sunk.
> >
> > I can't tell positively
> > Where her battered hulk may lie,
> > Nor name one individual

Who put her there to die.

She started on this fatal voyage
November twenty-fifth,
And on my word, by April third,
Her last salt air she sniffed.

I think his name was Sanders,
The guy they put in charge.
They didn't know his C.P.O.
Was gotten on a barge.

Our crew was quite a mixture,
They came from far and near:
From Boston came the Humboldt Kid,
From California -- Skoro, Vladimir.

From the Midwest came Tom Flaherty,
To this boy foam meant thirst.
From Wisconsin Leland Jensen
Who came to be an Ensign
Since it rhymes much better than 3rd or first.

There was speech like that of Willow's –
So round, so firm, so choice.
And that of Nealy Nelms
Giving orders to the helms
In his built-in high-doppler voice.

There were boys who really studied,
With books they were sublime:
Linsenmeyer with his Dutton,
And Lipsett with his Time.

With this conglomeration
They started on the run.
Oh it's true there were survivors,
There are 18 "still-alivers,"

But the dirty work's been done.

Can we put the blame on Allen
For chowing by the hour?
Or on mule driver Obley
Who pushed and shoved so nobly
As he raced into the shower?

Was it due to Bob Hart's travels
Every week in his Renault?
Was it because of Merrill Dubach,
With his flat hat nicely two-blocked,
Looking saltier than salt?

Can we put the blame on Jackson,
The pearl of Oyster Bay,
Who came here to New London
Without the benefit of Cape May?

Could it have been the men around us,
Who taught us everything thing,
From the rotors in our motors
To our ping-train-listen-ping?

Could it have that old Bob Freitag
Reflected too much light?
Or that young John Patrick Davey
Didn't think in Hooligan's Navy
He'd be marching left and right.

This is the last man – it's apropos –
For he has sorely been misnamed.
Not even *near* the Middle
Has he been since first he came.

Now there you have the villains
Who ran the ship aground,
The ones who really heard

That familiar crunching sound.

So remember this, you gentlemen
Of Class 3-53,
And all the men who follow you
Who wear the square OC,

She's a phantom ship you're sailing,
Whether monomoy or tug –
The Neversink has done been sunk –
You see – we pulled her plug.

The poem got a lot of laughs throughout and applause at the end. Some of the descriptions ("Lipsett with his Time") got "ah-has!" and moans from the instructors.

The next morning at graduation, there were a couple of speeches, one from Captain Julius Jacot, the Officer-in-Charge of Officer Indoctrination School, of which OCS was a part. After the speeches, we walked across the stage to receive a handshake from him.

He took my hand and held it.

"Mr. Connolly, I understand you wrote a poem about your class."

In the cloakroom after the commissioning dinner

"Yes, sir."

The captain kept me standing there for thirty seconds longer, he talking pleasantly and I nodding my head and saying mostly, "Yes sir." Finally I said, "Yes sir, I will," he shook my hand, we saluted and I left the stage and went to my seat.

After the ceremony I got questions. "What was that all about? Why did Jacot stop you?"

"He wants a copy of the poem."

Graduation Day, April 3, 1953, was Good Friday. The day we started was November 25, 1952, two days before Thanksgiving. Symbolically it should have been the other way around.

Ensign
Donald A. Connolly –
commissioning portrait

Chapter Four

San Francisco

On the 17th floor of the Appraisers Building on Sansome Street in downtown San Francisco, in the office of the director of the Rescue Coordination Center for the Commander, U.S. Coast Guard Western Area, the commanding officer was on the phone.

"Yeah, Pete, how you doing down there?"

He was talking to Mr. Peterson, the chief warrant officer who was the officer-in- charge of the Ft. Point Lifeboat Station, a Coast Guard unit located on San Francisco Bay between the Golden Gate Bridge and the Bay Bridge, a facility with small craft for rescue and general utility purposes.

"Tell you what – I got some blue-eyed ensigns here – just arrived. For indoctrination, training. They need to get some experience in what we do here. Can you help me?"

We ensigns standing near his desk, blue-eyed or not, weakly smiled, or smirked, or simply turned away. Another little dig at our being fresh-hatched. But it pretty well described the way we were – wide-eyed, innocent, inexperienced. Maybe trusting. At least he didn't say "baby-blue-eyed."

We were five: Dubach and I from Class 2-53, plus three others from the classes before ours, Lee Harrison who had driven me home at Christmas, Russ French and Sarge Horwood. (Sarge's full name was Sargent Pierce Horwood, so the combination "Ensign Sargent" sounded like a new rank.) We had arrived at various times in mid-April depending on whether or not we had taken leave in addition to travel time. Now we were all here and it was time to put us to work.

The Rescue Coordination Center was an impressive place: a large, two-story window-less room with a huge map of the Pacific Ocean from the west coast of North America to the coast of Asia covering one wall, displaying the land masses and islands with names and locations of U.S. military bases, and moveable symbols of ships, planes, and other units that could be utilized when coordinating a rescue.

This was designated as the Western Area in the Coast Guard command structure. The districts were smaller commands within the Area, each with defined boundaries and a headquarters: the 11th District headquartered in Long Beach, California; the 12th District in San Francisco; the 13th District in Seattle; the 14th District in Juneau, Alaska; and the 17th District in Honolulu. Each has a Rescue Coordination Center and handles its own events; when a rescue would encompass more than one district, the Area would get involved. The Area also figured in assigning personnel to the RCCs in those districts. There was an Eastern Area command headquartered in New York City that served the same purpose for Coast Guard activities in the Atlantic Ocean.

The size of the Center and the elaborate communications facilities exuded a sense of importance, even if much of the time nothing seemed to be happening, and even when it was, your involvement was pretty much as an onlooker. I heard one of the permanent staff, an officer a couple of grades above us ensigns, who was showing his in-laws the place, proclaim: "There's nothing between me and the orient!" Except, I was to learn, a number of RCC personnel in the turf-conscious districts.

"What I got in mind, Pete," the commanding officer continued, "they go to your place, the air station, and the 83s, a week each place, and two or three weeks here. One at a time—there're five of 'em. Then they can go to work."

As he listened to the response, we looked at each other – our indoctrination and training and duty had been laid out in five minutes.

"Great. Got to check with the other COs, but there shouldn't be any problem. They'll be there Monday, paperwork in hand."

Our living arrangements were up to us. Instead of government housing we were given a quarters' allowance. By the time I checked in for duty, Lee Harrison had already signed up an apartment, actually a "flat," in the Avenues west of downtown. It was a contingency arrangement, depending upon us late arrivals to agree. Dubach was married and would find his own housing. So in the apartment there would be the other four of us, Russ, Sarge, Lee, and myself.

At first sight the apartment was pretty barren, but the price was right and there was promise of more furniture from the landlord, Hal Stoll, a young family man with a new baby who lived in the flat above. It was an old place in the last stage of refurbishing, and he was anxious to start getting some revenue. A benefit of its age was the large size of the rooms, with a living room, full dining room and kitchen, plus three bedrooms, two small and one large.

May 6, 1953
Dear Mom, Jim and Gram,
... The apartment is beginning to look like something. More furniture all the time. The landlord is a swell guy who has been having a little rough time. His own apartment right above us isn't near as nice as ours because he's been fixing ours up to rent it, and we've got most of his furniture. We have a good gas stove, gas heat, and plenty of hot water.
...You'd really get a kick out of the way we live at the apartment. We are waiting for the packages from home so haven't bought much in the line of dishes, pans, etc. Every night we take down the drapes and use them for blankets. We eat soup with wooden spoons and forks. We bought one paring knife, and use that for all cutting. It's really funny sometimes.

Those are a few sentences from the earliest letter my mother saved. Certainly there were others before that, telling about my new life and duties. The experiences, military and otherwise, were building, piling one on another, and I found myself amazed and delighted, reveling that they were all wrapped in the aura of that beautiful city.

...Things are progressing slowly but surely. I've finished my week on the 83-foot patrol boats, and am now at a life boat station practically in the shadow of the Golden Gate Bridge.
Last week on the boats was pretty quiet so far as search and rescue was concerned, but I had a wonderful time.

Small boats in the Coast Guard are frequently identified by length—their identification numbers start with that dimension. In San Francisco Bay, there were three boats assigned to patrol and rescue duties, each taking a three-day shift, stationed on the waterfront at the local landmark, Fisherman's Wharf. The morning was typically cool and gray when I showed up at Pier 47, the first of our group to be assigned to the 83s. It was the 83370, McQueeny's boat – Ensign Michael J. McQueeny from Kansas City, Missouri, red-haired and round-cheeked with eyes and a smile that welcomed you warmly. Like most "older" junior officers, he knew the sense of innocence, ignorance and hesitation a new ensign would feel, and he took pains to instruct me in everything they were responsible for, even if they weren't doing it at the moment.

CG 83370 at Pier 47, San Francisco, California

That week on the 83s gave a special dimension to my growing enchantment with The City. I saw it from a seaman's point of view, almost *in* the Bay, at eye-level just above the fish, traveling across its expanse, passing sights I'd only read about, and feeling part of a friendly group with a meaningful mission. The two gorgeous bridges, Alcatraz Island (still a functioning penitentiary at the time), the bay-side towns of Sausalito and Tiburon and Alameda, even the working areas of the San Francisco waterfront with its fishing boats and merchant ships – all of them pushed my button of being in a special time and place.

I had been in San Francisco once before – *through* the city, to be more accurate – for one night, in a cheap hotel, in September 1951. That summer I worked in the woods of Idaho for a U.S. Department of Agriculture forestry project, and was traveling on railroad passes, courtesy of my father's employment at the

Wabash Railroad. Instead of returning to St. Louis by the route I had come, I decided to go by way of Los Angeles to see an aunt and uncle and some family friends. That meant changing trains in San Francisco with the possibility of seeing a cousin in the Marines stationed in the area. She wasn't available and it was late and I was cautious, so I got something to eat and went to bed, heading south the next morning.

San Francisco has been described as one of the few unique cities in the country – Boston, New York and New Orleans were the others mentioned. ("All the rest are Cleveland.") That reputation is rightly deserved and needs no support from me. Just standing at the foot of Market Street, the Bay and the Bay Bridge in one view, the Golden Gate in another, streets climbing the hills in still another, mountains in the distance, and, if you're lucky, blue sky with scudding white clouds above, makes one glad to be alive, and be there. Even in the frequent fog, maybe *especially* in the fog, the city can become breathtaking and exciting. When viewed from the Top of the Mark, the famous lounge and restaurant on the nineteenth floor of the Mark Hopkins hotel perched high on Nob Hill, the finger of fog slipping under the Golden Gate Bridge in the evening hours pointing across the bay, by nighttime filling it and the city with glistening droplets, casts a spell that tends toward enchantment. I experienced that view early in my stay and came to enjoy it often.

During my week on the 83s, it was the small fishing boats that gave us most of our work. We would receive a radio call from one of them – they all knew our radio frequencies by heart – saying they had broken down or were in some situation that needed a tow or some kind of assistance. One of them proved to be my undoing.

All the skippers were really great. I wrote you about McQueeny, the first one I was with. The next two were just about as nice. Anderson, the second one, is about 30, but nice for an <u>old</u> man. Flugelman was the last one, exactly the same age as McQueeny, who is his roommate. It was on Flugelman's boat that we went outside "the gate" into the Pacific after a small fishing boat that had broken down.

The Pacific is noted for being rough in these parts, and I felt the full effect. McQueeny had been kidding me about going outside the gate and getting seasick; but said that it is nothing to be ashamed of, just go to the rail and let it come.

The part of the Pacific just outside the Golden Gate is called "The Potato Patch," named after a rough, serrated ocean bottom that sends up line after line of bumpy waves you can't avoid and can't help feel, especially in a small craft. A fisherman was out pretty far, his engine had died, and he needed a tow back to home port inside the bay. It was around noon and our midday meal was ready to be served – steak and all the trimmings.

As our boat headed out the Gate, I joined the crew at the mess table below decks, supposedly a stable part of a boat, but at this time also a stuffy part. As the meal progressed the bump-bump-bumpbump from the Patch continued hitting us, and my stomach started to churn. I left the table and went topside into the fresh air. Deep breathing didn't help. Nor did the plate of meat scraps and fat that the cook set on the deck for the ship's pet dog. The sun was bright and the meat shone in all its greasy glory. I closed my eyes and tried to will the whole situation away. When I opened them, one of the crew was sitting across from me, eating dessert – a piece of cake topped with a thick layer of icing.

Flugelman was on the bridge (not very far away on these boats), and when he saw my ashen face he jumped down and was at my side in a moment. He led me to a safe place at the stern where the wind would blow everything away from the boat.

[He] told me the same thing [as McQueeny], and when I did start to get sick, he was just like a mother to me. Said, "Don't feel bad, please, it happens to everybody. I'll leave you alone – I always like to be alone when I feel like that." I couldn't help laugh at his solicitude, although I appreciated it very much.

If I was laughing, it was mentally, or way after the fact.

Nobody snickered, only smiled knowingly as I made my way slowly to a spot where I could rest. Or maybe my laughter came, sardonically, when we moved back into the bay and the boat we were towing started its engine, threw off our tow line, gave us a wave and sped off to its home port under its own power.

That was my first lesson in doing our job regardless of what we might suspect will be a deceitful mission. But the most impressive lesson was how caring a group of hard-edged guys could be when, commission or not, a blue-eye was in trouble.

Life in the Apartment could have been the inspiration for the play "The Odd Couple."

Russ was given the name "Mother Russ" by the rest of us—thin, quiet, totally focused on orderliness, he fussed over dishes left in the sink or newspapers not properly disposed of. He was very good at following orders and expected everyone else to be just as dedicated. Most of his conversation was spent analyzing anything you said that seemed outside of his idea of order. My playfulness and tendency to exaggeration for the sake of a joke or a good story, he never understood.

Sarge was a responder, a short, slender student-type who listened a lot and spoke tentatively when he did, usually with a slight laugh. He never made a fuss, but seldom contributed anything original to an event. He took most things on "a slow bell." He seemed sheltered, unfamiliar with anything beyond day-to-day living, but anxious to expand his experience. At the Life Boat Station, he encountered his first dead body; a man had jumped from the Golden Gate Bridge and killed himself. Sarge said he helped pull the corpse from the water, that he needed to do that.

Lee was the creative type – an artist with boundless energy, cheerful, unpredictable and personally undisciplined. He was bulky-looking which belied his restlessness, his need to always be on the move. Just before our transfer west, he took leave and went home to Illinois, but stayed there only a day or two and went on to New York.

Looking back, I suppose my label would say an upbeat guy, extrovertish and optimistic, probably naïve, who went along with what seemed best for the group – until obviously being imposed upon. Or unacceptably challenged.

The largest bedroom had two single beds, and each of the other bedrooms had one. Russ wanted his own room. Sarge said he didn't care. Maybe because we both were from the St. Louis area and had known each other from the Washington University musical, the two noisy guys, Lee and I, wound up sharing the largest bedroom. That proved to be a challenge.

As a roommate, Lee turned out to be a slob. Our beds were pushed against opposing walls, which left an aisle between them. The other furniture consisted of a chest of drawers apiece – for clothes you *didn't* hang up. And we had a closet apiece – for clothes you *did* hang up. At least, that was the common understanding, I thought.

Lee seemed to have no idea what either item was used for. The floor was closer, faster, and more convenient than any clothes hook. A corner of the room was perfect for piling up dirty shirts, socks and underwear. His chest of drawers soon was piled high with "stuff." Near the window, on his side I'll admit, there was an easel and a kit of oil paints and brushes. A portrait was started but soon abandoned, or "in abeyance" while he figured out what to do with it. The clutter soon made its way over much of the space we shared.

It was obvious he wasn't going to change his habits. Talking about the mess and pointing out the smells from his paints and his clothes didn't impress him. So I drew a line down the middle of the room – his side and my side. He could do anything he wanted on his side, just don't let any of his clothes or shoes or toiletries or painting stuff get onto my side. It was a friendly truce; he was always so cheerful it couldn't be otherwise.

Tuesday, May 12, 1953
Dear Mom,
    The package arrived sometime last week, but as no one was here, I had to pick it up when I came home from the life boat station on Mon-

day. It is fine. Each of us has a single bed – three were furnished, and we bought a slightly damaged mattress with matching box spring for $40. I'm not sure how to describe it, but anyway, it's a complete bed and brand new. The landlord will probably buy it from us when we leave. He has said as much. And if not, over the months the cost will be negligible. About sheets – we are renting sheets from a linen company. Costs $2.50 per month – 2 sheets and pillow case a week. So don't send any sheets. Also, forget about sending any silverware — the cost of sending would probably be greater than what I could buy for out here. We got some from one guy's folks, which will do for a while.

...

Well, I didn't have good luck the whole time on the 83-footers. The last day I got sick – but I think I told you that, didn't I. Anyway, last week nothing like that happened at the Lifeboat Station. Nice bunch of fellows, so I enjoyed myself. And I learned something about boats, and about people.

US Coast Guard Station, Ft. Point, San Francisco, California.

It was easy to go to work for a week at Ft. Point Lifeboat Station. It's located between the two bridges, right on the water, a spot most visitors would gladly pay to experience. There wasn't a lot of rescue or patrol activity that week, but the boats had to be inspected and tested, and the imaginative boatswains and enginemen could always find a need to go to Alameda or check a ship on the other side of the bay.

The two memorable people at the station were the officer-in-charge, CWO Peterson and the senior enlisted man, Engineman First Class Brennan. Mr. Peterson came and went a lot, trusting Brennan to handle any assignments. His favorite word was "bullshit."

Brennan knew his job, did it well, and happily showed us the ropes and guided our experiences as best he could. He had been with Sarge the week before when the dead body was pulled out of the water, and Sarge felt a specially affinity for him.

This week, tomorrow, I go to the Air Station. The fellow who just came back from there didn't like it, said they aren't very friendly. A lot of times it seems the enlisted men are more friendly than the other officers are, especially if they are a couple of ranks above you. At the air station, there are more officers than enlisted men.

The Air Station, as advertised, was not pleasant or memorable. The guys there were "fly boys" with responsibilities they took seriously and routines they didn't like to break. We Blue-Eyes were a distraction and a disruption. So we watched what went on, asked questions, read some manuals – that kind of thing. I don't recall being flown in any aircraft, not even a patrol helicopter. Such a view of the city would be memorable.

On Friday, the last day of my week there, we had scallops for our principal meal at noon. I had never eaten scallops before. Only a few months before I had tasted my first lobster in New London. It was delicious and I was willing to try another "exotic" seafood.

My ride back to the city from the Air Station, located at the San Francisco airport south of the city, was by public bus. It was crowded and stuffy. I sat in the back and as the long ride progressed my stomach began to feel queasy. In the city, I walked from the terminal to the Coast Guard office on Sansome Street to see if any of my colleagues might be finished and ready to go home. My expression and coloring must have been on the green side because someone asked if I felt okay. I had to admit I didn't, and a moment later I was in the men's room vomiting.

My gut was painful and the Officer of the Day said I should go to the Public Health Service hospital and get checked out, that maybe it was food poisoning. My colleague – Sarge, I think – went with me in a Coast Guard vehicle. The hospital is a big place, serving a large retired military population, plus merchant seamen and active-duty Coastguardsmen. The Coast

Guard uses Public Health facilities and personnel for its health care.

Sarge helped me to the admissions desk in the main lobby. The time was early evening by now, and there was one person sitting behind the counter. He looked up at me as I bent over and rested my head on the cool marble, groaning the whole time. I told him what had happened and he got out a form to take my particulars. My answers were interspersed with moans and groans. When I pleaded for some kind of treatment before the vomiting returned, he said he was only a clerk and the hospital corpsmen were busy at the moment.

As if on cue, two corpsmen returned to the area, carrying a very large television set. At that stage of technical development, television sets were very bulky, and large-screen versions were especially huge, with a lot of extra framing to protect the electronics inside. They were bringing the television set to the desk so they could watch a Friday night championship boxing match that was about to start; they would get to me as soon as the television was set up and working.

Eventually, they took me to a treatment room to check vital signs for the doctor who was on duty. He was somewhere in the hospital.

I wasn't the first patient in that room that day. On the floor was mess of dried vomit, with some blood in it. Probably a seaman with an ulcer, from drinking, the corpsman said. The doctor arrived and examined me; by now my stomach was more tired than painful, and the doctor agreed that it might have been the scallops and maybe the stuffy bus that had combined to make me sick. It was probably nothing serious.

But, if I wanted, I could stay in the hospital, just in case. It would mean being there for the weekend—there was no doctor on duty who could release me until Monday.

Somehow I began to feel better. Much better. Sarge and I went home.

Thursday, May 28
Dear Mom, Gram and Jim,
I got the package okay – I think I told you. By the way, about

the sheets. You can send them – 2 for a single bed. I'll wash one a week, the bottom one. That'll save about 50 cents a week.

This is the last week of moving from place to place. Next week we start watches at the office. (A "watch" is merely the period of time you are on duty. The day is divided into 3 watches, 8 hours each, starting at midnight, 8 a.m. and 4 p.m.). The new schedule doesn't look too enjoyable, however. We are on one watch for 7 straight days, then off 2, then on the next watch for 7 days, off 2, etc. Often however, things pop us to change the schedule, and that may happen to us. It couldn't get any worse.

I was not meant to be a "watch-man." You need to be able to change your body's basic rhythms, like when you get tired and when you need sleep, so you can sleep in the daytime and be alert all night long. During my first few night watches, I wound up at a desk with my head in my hands struggling to stay awake. Military regulations required it; common sense demanded it. If you're going to do the job you're training for, you learn to take your turn standing the night watch. Maybe if you go from a week of day watches to a week of evening watches and then to a week of night watches you can handle the gradual switch. But then, you get two days off after each watch – what are you supposed to do, spend those days as if you're on your up-coming schedule?

I was falling asleep and got chewed out; I had tried to sleep before work, but couldn't do it. There wasn't much going on in the place, and there were plenty of others to handle the routine stuff, and we trainees weren't supposed to coordinate anything, but it was the principle of the thing. And the practical aspect of being able to do the job. The duty officer – "nothing between me and the orient" – didn't spare my feelings in front of everybody in the office. He eventually seemed to understand, and I did better as the week went on, but it was embarrassing, and more important it was disturbing to me.

The center was populated by the usual experienced, competent types who worked together but apparently seldom if ever socialized. There were several chief petty officers who had seen sea duty and were there as a finale before retiring. One chief had taken to shore duty enthusiastically and expanded his waistline significantly. Another chief carried a brief case to and from work every day; it contained his lunch. A young chief, Bowman, a career coastguardsman, was a contrast to his older counterparts and was happy to engage us in official and non-official chatter.

Another contrast to the older career enlisted was the aerographer, Ron Garrigues, a local boy serving out his enlistment. Ron was an artist, tall but a bit slouched, a would-be hippy encased in bell bottoms, who spontaneously drew cartoonish faces and characters; I still have one he sent to me in the Pacific, showing me berserk on a deserted island. Ron was out-going and non-military, but was able to portray the appropriate demeanor and perform the required duties. Being local he could guide us to restaurants and recreation, even arrange a date for me with a friend of his sister.

I don't know if all of us four approved of the fraternization that ensued with Bowman and Garrigues and a few other enlisted types. But we obviously enjoyed their personalities and company; they and their wives show up in photos at our parties.

Well, we finally had our first party. It was purely on the spur of the moment. This past Monday we found that all four of us were home together, so we decided to fix a big meal. Harrison did the shopping and bought a roast and cake mix and other stuff. We've bought enough utensils to cook such food. The cake turned out pretty good, and the roast looked like it was coming along okay, so suddenly he suggested that we invite somebody over for dinner, preferably females. Only one hitch – we didn't know any. I called McQueeny, whose fiancée has 3 roommates. He couldn't come himself, but another ensign did and he rounded up 4 girls beside his own date. He was Flugelman, the guy who was so concerned when I got seasick. Altogether there were 10 for dinner. We had the roast, potatoes, carrots, deviled eggs, and a good salad that Harrison made. Also the cake. Had to use paper plates, and only 4 could have coffee at one time, but we managed. In fact, it was more fun that way. They stayed until 11:30, evidently enjoying themselves.

Three days after the letter above, I wrote the one below.

Things could happen fast when they had to. I wrote the letter at the office, on duty – it's typed and that was my only access to a typewriter.

Sunday
May 31

Dear Folks –
It's me again. But this time not so happily newsy.
We finally got the word that we are going to leave here, probably in 3 weeks. You have no idea how that really hurts – all of us were getting into the swing of this place, and beginning to meet people and really enjoy ourselves. But as I said while at home, I didn't know how long we'd be here.
You probably also remember that I said we might go somewhere out in the Pacific. Well, that was as true a statement as I ever made. The notice came in last night and as yet is not officially divulged. It said that by June 22 or by 2 months after beginning training, we are to be assigned to the various places: 1 person to Seattle, 1 to Midway Is., 2 to Guam, and 1 to Sangley Point, Philippines (right near Manila). No one knows where he will go – that's up to the head guys at the office. However, they may ask us which we prefer, but even then, what we prefer may not have anything to do with it. As it stands, it seems that Dubach will probably go to Seattle, since he is married; the other 4 of us would be willing to give it to him. So I will probably wind up out in the Pacific; where, I don't know and right now, don't give a damn.
So, FORGET about the sheets and tell Aunt Ceil to forget about her stuff too. And decidedly I won't need any more clothes. I'm wondering what to do with all I've got with me now.
Please don't get shook up about this. I don't know when I'll leave, or if I can come home first. Perhaps it wouldn't be wise to come home, since I had been there such a short time ago. The leave could be better used later. That's all for now; just sort of an advance notice. Will write details when I get them.
Love, Don

Deep down I did give a pretty big "damn." The specialness of this place had worked its spell on all of us and we spoke about the super-remote possibility of staying here, at least one of us, serving out our two years of service assigned to the Rescue Coordination Center, Western Area, San Francisco, California. Not likely, but well, just maybe. Wasn't somebody going to retire? Or be transferred? Maybe – die?

I was into the swing of the watches.

I was going to plays and musicals at the Geary Theatre, taking a date to the Purple Onion to hear the Kingston Trio, being introduced by McQueeny to exotic food at India House restaurant.

I had opened a checking account and joined a fitness gym.

I had come to know the neighborhood barber.

In the spirit of the city, I took a small step toward the independent judgment college is supposed to instill. The movie "The Moon Is Blue" had opened there to much controversy, as it had all over the country, because it was "condemned" by the Legion of Decency, the Catholic office with a lot of power over the film industry. I knew the play by John van Druten which was a hit on Broadway and couldn't imagine how that story could be handled to get that rating. After some thought I went to see it, and came out even more bewildered: the word "virgin" was used (supposedly a no-no) and there was dialogue to the effect: He: "Don't you think you're too preoccupied with sex?" She: "Isn't that better than being occupied with it?" If this was an official Catholic evaluation and I was interested in getting into this field, I would have to look into it.

I was making and visiting friends all over the Bay Area.

When I went to the Coast Guard personnel office in Alameda across the bay to check in, I ran into Galen Nielsen, a chief who had been at OCS in a class or two after ours. A gentle but active and athletic person, he was playing basketball when I sprained my ankle and was the one who assisted me to the infirmary. Being a knowledgeable chief he was helpful to the pre-Blue-Eyes in his class. Somehow he ran afoul of one of the instructors who apparently questioned his "adaptability," and eventually he was dismissed from OCS. Those who knew him found this unbelievable, but the decision stood.

We renewed our friendship in that office, and cemented

it during my stay on Flugelman's 83-boat where he was the engineman. Before leaving the area I spent many pleasant times with him and his wife, Louise, and their new baby. They even brought the baby to one of our parties, giving us singles a taste of the future.

I learned there were relatives in Oakland and went to see them.

The party Sunday with the Connolly's was fine. It was a birthday party for the oldest and youngest brothers, I found out. About 10 were there. Just for the afternoon – had buffet supper and sat around and talked. The oldest, Clem, knew Dad and Uncle Fred (from the army). I showed them the pictures I had.

And there were "friends of friends." A priest from the University, when he learned I was going to San Francisco, gave me the names and address of relatives south of San Francisco. "Very nice people," he assured me, "they'll enjoy meeting you." I got in touch with them and they invited Sarge and me for a Sunday dinner.

The chauffer met us at the bus station in an old green Cadillac. The two boys, about 11 and 9, were with him. As soon as we got to the house, which is in the most fashionable part of San Mateo, we were ushered to the swimming pool to meet the folks. The husband is an M.D; the wife is about 35 or 40, but really well, well preserved. (I can hear the old girl [Mom] now, "She never has to do any work." True, true.) So we spent the afternoon at the pool, which by the way, is heated to take the chill off.

The house is one of those spacious affairs, not new at all. Very plain interior, a kind of Spanish tinge, but with pointed roof and all. Huge fireplace and dining room with windows all over it. We had dinner around 5:30, and a little later Mrs. Stephens' mother came home from making a retreat, and we met her. She had a friend with her, and had the chauffer drive the friend to S.F. As long as the car was coming this way, we went along too.

It was a most eventful day in what had been an uneventful existence socially. They were most hospitable, not at all affected by the dough. They have 4 kids, a daughter 13, the two boys, and a baby boy 1 year old. It was quite a domestic scene; except for the physical surroundings, I might just as well have been at home.

Three weeks after the initial notice of our pending reassignments, the official and final paperwork came.

19 June 1953
Dear All,
We got the word finally. Our duties here will end July 6. We'll have a couple of days to clear things up I guess, and then we'll go to Honolulu for a month. After the month, we'll [Sarge and I] go to Guam. While in Hono I'll be getting $9 a day plus my regular salary. Out of the $9 I'm supposed to pay for my room and board. Usually it's possible to save quite a bit of it. The month in Hono is something I hadn't bargained for – and should be pretty nice.
… I'll send some of my warm clothes home in my gray suitcase. My cool sport clothes I'll take along.

All four of us at the apartment were scheduled for Honolulu and then points west. Dubach was assigned to Seattle. Russ French would go to Midway Island, and Lee Harrison to Sangley Point. We could take leave first if we wanted to; there was no rigid indoctrination plan in Honolulu, just exposure to that district's units and how we might operate at our new station. Harrison decided to take leave; French, too, as I recall. It would be Sarge and I making our way together and without the others. Maybe the idea of glamorous, romantic Honolulu pushed aside the reality of our final destination – Guam, a small, undeveloped spot on the far side of the Pacific, close to nothing civilized – but I didn't think much about it. I knew it had been a major location in World War II against the Japanese and was totally devoted to the U.S. military, a tropical spot just north of the equator. It was what it was, and I'd make the most of it; other guys had served the same duty and survived. And thrived? Well, who knew? You do what you gotta do.

On July 15 I penned two letters ("penned" —no typewriter! – must buy one in Honolulu).

Dear Folks —

Nothing new. No definite date as to the day we leave. Should be within the next 3 days, however. Since last Saturday I've been getting $9 a day above my regular salary and food allowance. If that continues while in Hono, I should wind up with a hundred or so extra. However, Hono is pretty expensive, just to live, with no "luxuries."

I'm enclosing 2 keys. The small one is for the gray suitcase – the large one is a key to our house which I found in my pants.

We've rented the apartment, so I got my $30 advance rent back. We can stay here until we leave, so we are spared moving out early to make room for the new tenants. They are 4 girls – bad timing, eh what?

The landlord had us [Sarge and me] up for dinner the other night. He's quite a guy. Has this apartment rented, and also the new one below – now he's thinking of selling the building.

So much this time. Next time should be from the islands.
It was good talking to all of you.
Love, Don

That sounds like I was going to dive off the high board into murky waters and not surface for a long time. Still, to a Blue-Eye, it was a dramatic, maybe romantic move.

Wed
July 15 --
Dear Mom –

I just wrote a letter to home – sent the keys I told you about... Some of the clothes I sent home are dirty. Shirts, especially. Tell Jim he can wear any of them if he wants. Bob, too. I've got white shirts there I'll never wear; they might as well get used up.

It will be impossible for me to see Gene [my brother the priest in Los Angeles]...We have to be here at the apartment every day between 10 a.m. and 1 p.m. so the Navy can get in touch with us if they want to. One day soon they'll call, and the next day we'll be gone. They never know very far in advance when we'll leave, so any long jaunt would be out of the question.

Much of the rest of the letter deals with my mother's distress that sons Gene and Jim aren't including their widowed mother in important goings-on in their lives. Gene had had a kidney removed and didn't tell her for a while; Jim was over 30, living at home with his mother and grandmother, and...

My analysis for her:

...With Gene it seems to be the idea of suffering in silence. ... With Jim, well, he just wants to have secrets. Nothing sinister, you understand ... I wouldn't worry about it from either of them. They are big boys now, and maybe have good reasons; each one has his own problems and in trying to work them out, often might seem to hurt another. But I believe it's unintentional....so just bear with them both in their little oddities and enjoy yourself in the meantime. You're not the first mother to feel that way.

So much for the sermon.

... This will end it now. The medal arrived okay. Thank Father Charles for me. Be good.

Love, Don

On the afternoon of July 17, Sarge and I presented ourselves, orders in hand and luggage at our feet, to the Naval Air facility on the far side of the bay in Alameda for transportation to Hawaii. We were on the Bay because our transportation was a MARS Flying Boat, a large, bulky structure (like a boat!) with wings and four propeller engines. The Boat would use San Francisco Bay as its takeoff strip.

Galen and Louise Nielsen with the baby came to see us off. After becoming good friends in a short time, we now had the prospect that it would be a long time before we would be together again.

Sarge and I checked in and went aboard and settled into our seats. As I recall, the body was a double-decker, with two levels of passenger space. Eventually the plane taxied into the bay to prepare for its takeoff. Evening was closing in and lights on the two bridges popped on, stringing a sparkling necklace across the bay. Or was it a chain that would block our departure? How would this slow-moving beast overcome the drag from the water and pick up speed and dodge the bridges and get itself into the air?

The Flying Boat lumbered to the far end of the bay and turned around so it was heading west, toward the bridges. It started its move forward, engines revving and straining, barely rising from the water; suddenly there was an explosive roar, and a burst of fireworks spewed from each wingtip. It was JATO propulsion – a Jet-Assisted Take-Off. Those jets pushed our nose up and lifted the plane quickly up and over the Bay Bridge before they burned out.

It was a spectacular finale to a magical time in a special city which lay below and eventually behind us in the distance, its lights twinkling their 'good-bye' before the fog rolled in.

Chapter Five

War as War

It didn't occur to me, as we left the U.S. mainland and headed into the Pacific, that we were getting closer to the war. My assignment was on Guam, far from the action. My branch of service was the Coast Guard, not likely to be involved in any combat. The war had been going on for three years and, in the last two years, the action had become pretty stalemated. Everyone was expecting it to be over soon. On July 11, 1953, before we left San Francisco, it was.

At least an armistice was signed on that date. The peace would be supervised by an international commission as details were worked out. Officially, the war still has not ended. As I write this in 2014, no treaty has been signed.

So, as I headed west, toward the war, there wasn't a war zone.

There had been terrible battles – Pork Chop Hill and Heartbreak Ridge and Chosin Reservoir, just three of the better known – and loss of life. The killing, maiming, and mental battle scars, the cost, the turmoil to our society – I was aware of these and lamented them all. Several friends had been drafted and were serving somewhere in Korea, but seemed to be in no danger.

The reality of the war came close to me in the summer of 1951. While working in the forests of Idaho, I met the Rowland family from the nearby town of Headquarters. On a Sunday morning they picked me up hitchhiking to the town of Pierce; we were all heading to Mass at Our Lady of the Woodland church. Their son, the oldest child, had been killed in the early fighting; it was obvious that Mrs. Rowland, especially, was in mourning. On Sundays during the summer, when there was Mass in Pierce, they picked me up on the road. Several times they invited me home for dinner and for some visiting with them and their two young daughters. For the summer I filled a missing piece of their family.

I had lived through World War II as a teen-ager. The St. Louis Post-Dispatch printed large maps of the European and Pacific battle areas and they adorned my bedroom wall with my markings that showed the progress. With the Boy Scouts, I collected newspapers and scrap metal, and served as an aide to an air raid warden during exercises to test our nighttime blackouts. In 1942, I started working in a neighborhood grocery store and became intimate with food rationing (collecting the stamps from customers, counting the piles of the red and blue pieces to get our next shipment of meat and canned goods). My oldest brother went to the Army Air Corps and at war's end was stationed in Japan; another brother was drafted late in the war and served as an office clerk at the Pentagon.

With World War II there was a sense of unity in the country – pull together, get it done – because it was necessary to win, to defeat the evil that our enemies represented. When it ended, we were all happy that we had "saved the world," and now we could get on with our lives. I was almost fifteen when it ended and the future lay brightly before me.

Then, in 1950, just five years later, came Korea. Its beginning was sudden, unexpected. Each person my age could only wonder how it would affect them. Would it be kept small and localized and not involve a lot of us? Would it be over quickly or drag on? Nationally, the Korean War was different from World War II. The political reactions were divided. The nation did not unite behind it – officially it was a Police Action, not a war, under the umbrella of the United Nations, but the U.S. seemed to be bearing the brunt. With World War II so close in memory, people were tired of war.

"Why are we fighting there?"

The Korean War has been called The Forgotten War, eclipsed by the broader and stranger conflict in Viet Nam, and then by the wars in the Middle East. Memorials are still being planned and built, in Ohio, for example, as survivors insist on recognition. Although a late entry, the Korean War Memorial on the Mall in Washington is a striking and meaningful reminder of the slogging and misery of that particular conflict. It shows a patrol of nineteen servicemen in combat gear crossing what might be a rice paddy; they represent the four Defense Department services (the Coast Guard is not included). It records the number of personnel killed: 54,246 from the United States and 628,833 designated as United Nations. The total wounded was 103,284 U.S. and 1,064,453 U.N.

That's a lot of people, most of them young. As I was.

The memorial bears the inscription: "Our nation honors her sons and daughters who answered the call to defend a country they never knew and a people they never met."

There were a lot of heroes. Certainly not me. I felt fortunate to be able to fulfill an obligation, maybe contribute something, and still not be in harm's way. With my education behind me and my career (whatever that would be) ahead of me, my being "in the war" wasn't uppermost in my mind. I felt in an enviable situation, and optimistic: "It'll work out okay."

So I waded in.

Chapter Six

Honolulu

Sat night
July 18, 1953

Dear Mom and all –
Arrived here in Honolulu this morning after a 12 ½ hour flight. Came in a Mars flying boat – most comfortable and enjoyable. Slept almost all the way.
Am staying at the Elks Club, where most of the transient CG officers stay. It's right by Waikiki beach, where I went swimming today. Sarge Horwood came over with me. Two others, Middleton and Obley (who were in New London with me) have been here a week or so. Obley is to be here permanently, but Middleton goes to Manila. They received their training in NY, like I did in Frisco.
We are going to rent a car and see the island of Oahu. Get out a map so you can see just where Honolulu is. The city itself is just like any other old town – dirty, narrow streets, small shops and bars, and in this case, plenty of sailors.
Out here on Waikiki it is beautiful. Our 'lodge' juts out on a point of land and the ocean comes right below our big balcony. There is always a breeze from the ocean that both cools you and spreads the fragrance of the flowers around.
I'll take some pictures and send them home.
This is all for now. I'm very tired.
Love, Don

In February 1995, Barbara and I visited Honolulu; it was the first return for both of us – Barbara worked there as a nurse in 1953-54, the same time I was there!

Of course the city had changed; we had expected it to. But what had made it special in our time there – its relaxed atmosphere, the openness of the beaches and access to the hotels on Waikiki – was diminished if not totally gone. We managed to have a drink "under the banyan tree" at the Moana Hotel on

Waikiki, but we had to work our way through the maze of shops that line Kalakaua Boulevard and block the Moana from sight. There's still a lot of beauty on the island, and the climate can't be beat, but the city of Honolulu was jammed, noisy, and generally unpleasant.

Or was it just that almost forty years had intervened?

A special disappointment during that visit was the absence of the Elks Club where Sarge and I stayed. It was old then, and its age reflected the feeling of a tropical land that was gone even then. Photos in my album show our room with a mix of leather and rattan chairs, small tables draped with non-matching cloths, light sconces high on the wall, and a horizontal diamond-shaped mirror over a marble basin-and-backsplash supported on spindly metal legs. There were trim and garnishes everywhere. Across the narrow porch was the Pacific, unobstructed except for the ornate railing. Sarge and I called it "The Somerset Maugham Room."

Our room at the Elks Club, Honolulu, 1953 – the 'Somerset Maughm Room'

There's a new Elks Club there now, modern, of course. The old one was termite-ridden and full of decay. It had to be torn down.

As in San Francisco, our duty time was spent visiting CG units and being in the RCC during daytime hours – no night watches here, thank God! There wasn't anything for us to do, so we knew our stay in Honolulu would be brief. And that meant we had to make the most of our free time.

In the letter above I asked my mother to contact a high school friend who had been in plays and worked on the school newspaper with me. He went to Notre Dame and on several occasions I met his roommate, Don Machado, from Honolulu, and I asked my mother to get Machado's phone number or address from my school mate.

Friday
July 31, 1953

Dear Mom – et al!
Your letter arrived yesterday or the day before. I called Machado and he was glad to hear from me. I'm going to a Japanese feast with his father tonight. Don himself is preparing to take the Hawaii bar exam and his mother is busy, so they can't go. The feast is in honor of a Japanese baseball team that is here now to play the Hawaiian team. The father [a sports writer] had 2 tickets, so asked if I wanted to go. Also, I'm invited to their house tomorrow night for dinner.

This was a long letter with a lot of family stuff, and I put it aside when it was time to go to the feast.

This is written 4 hours after I began – just got back from the feast. It was really Japanese. Sat on cushions on the floor, ate with chopsticks (for the first time). The food was plentiful and various – chicken, a couple kinds of rice, salad, shrimp, barbecued pork, squid, pineapple and watermelon. All this was fixed Japanese style. No wonder the Japanese aren't fat – they can't eat fast with chopsticks.

What made the dinner special, and the reason Don's father wanted to go, was that the Japanese team was the first to visit Hawaii since World War II. There was concern about the reception they would receive. But even with the language barrier the hosts managed to set a cordial tone and there was no sign of anger or resentment

Some of the family stuff in the letter:

I plan to buy a portable typewriter soon. I was hoping to get it through the PX, but they don't save very much on typewriters. There's a good Swiss model downtown that looks good – it's cheaper than most U.S. models and better in operation.

After I pay for the typewriter, I'll send the rest of the money home. I've got about $450 in the bank. I'll send about $350 home. I owe you for June and July – so you can keep $50 and put the rest in the bank. Or maybe buy bonds with it – whichever gets the most interest. Also, I'll start making an allotment out so you can put my money away – but I'll take care of that later.

Jim – I dropped in to see Rex Revelle at his gym the other day. Honolulu isn't very large, and once you are in downtown you are close to everything. It was a pleasant visit – he talked a lot about [big names in the bodybuilding world]. Has a nice gym – and of course is well built. But he must be getting old – even the hair on his chest is getting gray. I'll enclose one of his cards.

I'm taking a course in German from USAFI (see Jim). Horwood and I are taking it together, since we'll be on Guam a long time, probably with nothing to do. Also, as I might decide to go to school in Europe when I get out, it would come in handy – yes, I've been thinking about it, and probably will – but don't worry about that now.

The big news that began this letter was about "the word":

We got the word. We leave here one week from today, Friday Aug 7. It'll take about 2 or 3 days to get to Guam, as the plane usually remains overnight at the various islands along the way. I'll have been here 3 weeks by then.

In the week that remained I bought the Hermes typewriter – it shows up in pictures of our Elks Club room. It had Elite type – the smaller font would put more words on the paper. That's what I figured; somehow that seemed important at the time.

So many people had been writing me letters and sending me stuff – for the apartment, for myself, for my morale – and entertaining me and anyone with me, I wanted to do something in response before we left Honolulu. It wasn't hard to find a store that catered to tourists wanting to take something back home, and there was the answer: an assortment of Hawaiian jellies went all my benefactors.

I also saw a lot of Machado that week. Later I wrote:

He took me to the homes of some of his friends, and less affected people I've never met. The day before I left, he and I went walking through the Hawaiian wilderness to see the "Sacred Falls," nothing special but it made an enjoyable hike.
I took him out to dinner one night.

And about the island itself:
It's pretty nice, but not exotic and tropical as the common concept of Hawaii usually is, or at least as mine was. The climate is wonderful – there's always a breeze blowing to keep it from becoming too hot, and yet it's warm enough to dress very casually, go without socks, or for that matter, go without shoes. There is a sign in the Sears store requesting patrons not wearing shoes not to use the escalator.

And a final sign-off from Honolulu:
So much for now.
Keep the faith – cut the grass.
Love,
Malihini (Newcomer) Don

Chapter Seven

There, and Getting There

Tomorrow will be one month on Guam. The time has passed quickly, as it usually does with new surroundings. It hasn't been unpleasant, as many said it would. But when we get into the swing of things, maybe time will weigh heavily upon us. That is the most plentiful commodity out here – time. The next is liquor.

That's how my journal begins, written on September 10, 1953, in longhand. Not on my new typewriter. There are nine pages written that way, maybe because I wrote them in the Rescue Coordination Center, waiting to stand watches. Maybe it was too rainy and moist in my "hut" to allow the paper to go through the typewriter carriage. The script is clear and without correction; that conjures up a lot of "maybe's".

The journal continues:

Sarge Horwood and I arrived on August 11, 1953 at NAS Agana, Guam. We had been in Honolulu 3 weeks, and before that, in San Francisco for about 2 ½ months. More about those places later, perhaps. The important thing is: we had arrived.

Sounds a bit MacArthur-ish, doesn't it? No doubt I was writing for the ages, anticipating a once-in-a-lifetime experience. The "perhaps" stayed just that: recalling and recording San Francisco and Honolulu has only happened in writing this story. Thank God for the letters my mother saved.

At CG Air Detachment, Wake Island. CG R5D plane

    The plane trip had lasted 3 days – Sat. to Tues. Lest it seem I can't count, remember that the International Dateline pokes its long, thin self somewhere between Midway and Wake. We left Barber's Point, Oahu, Saturday morning [August 8th-- engine trouble delayed us a day] and arrived about 12 hours later at Wake – Sunday evening. Only 45 minutes were spent at Midway to unload cargo and Russ French, another controller and our associate since April 25.

    Our flight westward was postponed a day due to the approach of Typhoon Nina on Guam. We got a chance to see a little of the island and rest up from the travel. Travel's funny – you sit all day and you're dead tired.

    We went swimming for about an hour. Used fins and goggles and were able to get a glimpse of the fish. The swimming 'hole' was a channel that just about cut the island in two – the water was clear and cool at that time, about 11 a.m. Later when the tide changes it develops a strong current and gets very hot.

    There is a CG Air Detachment on Wake – the only military installation on the island. I have since learned the convenience of such a set-up. The CG is a small, friendly and pretty informal outfit. These latter qualities stem from the first – its size. But when placed under the jurisdiction of a larger, more 'basic' organization [like the Navy], it loses a lot of its freedom.

    The boys on Wake were a fairly satisfied crew. Only 2 or 3 were there permanently – the others rotated every couple of weeks. There isn't much to do – during the day they make training hops, and at night there are movies and booze.

The controller who's stationed there taught me to play Acey-Deucey. I've forgotten how already.

We left Wake on Tuesday morning about 9. It was a clear beautiful day. It wasn't hot yet. The trip above the clouds was smooth and uneventful. I was reading "The Cardinal." I had finished "The Portrait of the Artist as a Young Man" just before, during the flight. What different books. One so human and heart-warming, the other so misguided. I must admit that Joyce does not attempt to paint the Church blackly. In fact, he states its teachings very well; but also cannot accept them. I think he is too proud – he lacks all sense of humility, and love. But he is an artist – his writing is artistically fine.

We began to hit the rain about 1:30 pm. Guam lay ½ hour away. With the rain came the lurching of the plane, and with that came the sympathetic vibrations of the stomach. The worst moments were the last: we made several passes at the landing strip – the clouds were thick, which made visibility poor, and the wind and rain were also of no assistance. The last minutes were too much for my terrestrial stomach – the water-proof paper bag that's tucked somewhere in each seat was brought forth. Sarge and I both prepared to use it. I wondered what would happen if we both lost the battle at the same time. I lost and Sarge won – that took care of that. We landed and skidded, something I had never done before. But it was land, wet as it was.

Our arrival was heralded by the beating of the rain – on the ground, on the bus, and on our hut. There are 2 seasons on Guam, they say –rainy and rainier. Which was this, I wondered. It rained all that night and practically all that week.

Our hut (all living quarters are called 'huts' on Guam) was "The Castle," Bachelor Officers' Quarters (BOQ) 5-24. Benny Weems, a pilot, was there to greet us – he was moving his clothes and other gear from the porch to one of the rooms. The porch was a dreary picture – the bed was in the middle, the deck [floor] was wet, and everything on the porch was moist. He was moving because it was too windy for him. Also too wet. It was a vulnerable spot in a slanting rain – the porch was screened halfway down on three sides, the lower half being horizontal slats which are slanted downward to keep out the rain and let in the breeze.

I took the porch and Sarge one of the rooms. It was comfortable enough. I managed to sleep well, although the moist sheets felt like starched lettuce leaves.

... After trying to get things settled a bit, Sarge and I went to the RCC to see just what we were in for for a year. We called first to tell them we were here. Chuck Lindberg was there, most happy to hear we had arrived. Between cloudbursts we went to the center – I think somebody drove us there.

It was located in a series of partially earth-covered Quonsets – it was air-conditioned! There were no windows, the floor was cement, and the lights were glaring. The drone of the air-cooling machinery is perennial, although the wonderful effects more than compensate for the noise.

Lindberg was in the middle of an incident. The typhoon had done its damage so far as RCC was concerned: the high seas had disabled a tug attempting to keep a transport off the breakwater, and a motor vessel, the Malaki, was missing. Don Mosiman, the other controller, had gone aboard the CGC Klamath when she stood out of the harbor to avoid the typhoon. He was aboard about three days – I didn't envy him.

Lindberg assured us that such an amount of business was rare and extreme. A month later I realize the truth of that statement.

We met Commander Robert McCaffery, our boss – grey-white hair, short, always attired in shorts and yellow sunglasses. I liked him from the beginning and have found my like well-grounded. He reminds me a lot of Dad, except he smokes cigars 10 times more than Dad ever thought of smoking. But he's fatherly – should be with four daughters.

Sarge is a great one for running into people he knows anyplace in the world. Guam was no exception. A football meeting was being held in the RCC – McCaffery was then the coach. Sarge walked up to one of the Navy ensigns around the table (a tall, heavy, rather bemused-looking individual) and said, "Did you go to Harvard?" Immediately I thought, "Oh my God, not again!" I didn't hear the rest of it, but the conversation established that they had both gone to Harvard, had mutual friends there and had at least seen one another around the campus.

Ray Davis ("Raymond H. J. Davis" to be precise) then became our unofficial guide to NAS Agana and other parts of Guam. Instead of dinner at the mess that night, he suggested we eat out. He selected the American Café – American in that it has a juke box with an abundance of Hank Snow records, is poorly lighted, and just as poorly appointed in the culinary arts.

It was raining so hard that the "gutters" along the road were flooded. From the road to the restaurant was a murky sea. Hunger being our driving force, we took off our shoes and waded to our first Guamanian meal. After dinner we drove to Tumon Beach which at that hour was nothing to see. Then "home" and to bed.

I began to wonder if having a car would be a plus. The air station was spread out on a hilltop, and the island itself was larger than I expected. Sarge had bought a used car in San Francisco, a pre-war Ford, something that he didn't care about bringing back, and it was being shipped. But most people didn't have cars. On the base there were plenty of busses on scheduled routes, and a lot of military and civilian cars and trucks that would give you a ride. I had gone through college without a car and had never really thought about having one "out here." Lindbergh didn't have a car and survived.

But Mosiman had an MG; he was the envy of all the young officers, especially since he had bought the jazzy car mostly with per-diem money he got because his orders or transportation had been messed up and he had a considerable delay, getting the extra money all the time, before arriving on Guam

It seemed that Ray had always had a car since the time he could drive and he didn't consider living without one, anywhere. I would have to wait and see.

My letters home now were typed on my own typewriter, in triplicate, so I wouldn't have to repeat myself to the brothers. After a short-and-sweet first one with my new address, the letters became pretty detailed.

18 August 1953
Dear Three –

Today is my first anniversary. One week on Guam. Rain has been my companion the whole time, making visits at least once a day, sometimes staying all day long. This is the rainy season, from now until the end of October or November. It keeps the grass and foliage a deep green and clothes and books slightly damp. We've got closets with light bulbs that burn continuously (called 'hot lockers') that keep things dry enough to prevent mildew. But the bed and pillow and cushions on the chairs are always sort of damp dry and smell sort of musty.

The place we live in is one of the better Quonset huts. The architecture out here shows a definite influence of the wartime school of construction. Ours, however, has the benefit of a large porch, which happens to be my room. It's open on three sides (screens, but no windows); as a result it's the windiest, and at times, the wettest.

The animal life here is different than most places. Ants are no bother – they're all over and there's nothing you can do about them. You do make an effort to keep the lizards out of the sink, though. At night the lizards congregate around the edges of the screen on the porch waiting for moths to land, attracted by the light. Then they creep out, usually two at a time, coming from opposite directions, for the kill. Look like two cars dead set on a collision. Usually they are pretty good; last night they got 14 out of 16. Not bad.

We haven't started standing watches yet, so I can't say how it will be. Our schedule will work out to 14 hours of work in every 96 hours – won't be hard to take. From what the boys here have said, there isn't very much to do during the working hours. That is, there isn't a lot of little stuff to take care of as in SanFran, but when there is a big incident, like a plane crash or a good-sized ship lost somewhere, there's plenty to do. Soon I should know.

Lindberg and Mosiman were most anxious for Sarge and me to take over the watches. They had been here almost a year and were anxious to leave. The time had passed rather quickly, they said. Mo had played tennis and had done some gambling, and one way or another had saved a good deal of money. He had also painted a picture or two from a kit. Chuck's interests lay in the same general 'pass-the-time' field. He had a fiancée at home who is Catholic; he isn't, and he was worried if it would work out. When he learned I was Catholic, he talked to me a lot about it, and when he left he sounded like he was going to go through with the marriage.

The first week they had us read publications that were supposed to be pertinent. Most likely they were – they make sense when you read them but the formality and heaviness of the style makes them hard to recall. That seems to be the fate of the military writer: he has a large audience, but is never well-remembered.

That first long letter of August 18 ended:

Life here is nothing to rave about, but it isn't too bad, either. The island is bigger than I thought (about 30 miles long and 5 miles wide) and there are plenty of people, about 60,000. Of course most are male military personnel. So far nothing in the opposite sex that would be of interest has appeared; probably won't, either, unless it's some Captain's daughter or a school teacher or something. There are library facilities and gyms and tennis courts and a golf course, and of course movies, to help pass the time. Soon, I hope, there will be a little theatre. If that gets going, I should have plenty to do. Soon I should know.

I'll close now, y'all. I'll be expecting replies shortly. My typewriter works fine; I've started my USAFI German course and it's going okay. I'm healthy, and fairly happy. Hope to stay that way. Be good, all of you.

Love, Don

Chapter Eight

Maybe, Maybe Not

"Soon, I hope, there will be a little theatre."

A Coast Guard Ensign, one week at a Naval Air Station on the way-out little island of Guam, and I'm talking about a little theatre? If it's going to be, it would have to be my doing. Maybe it was a "blue-sky" fantasy that only a "blue-eye" would put down on paper in a letter. But the words had also been spoken to others here, and like a genie let out of the bottle, they dispersed through the area and infected enough of the social fabric to get things started. Who could know where it would end?

In the first few days here I asked various people if there were any dramatics on the station, does anyone ever put on a play. The quick answer was usually a complete and final "no" but several said they thought there had been some interest. So-and-so said something about it once, but they weren't sure whether he was still around or not. One of the people I mentioned it to was our fourth controller, Lieutenant (junior grade) Paul Yost. He's an Academy man, a nice-looking, in-shape college wrestler, with a sense of humor and a pleasant but fairly serious personality. He didn't seem like the type who would be interested in something like this. He wasn't, but his wife was. That night Sarge, Mo and I went to visit the Yosts.

Paul's wife, Jan, turned out to be a very pretty blonde, hair worn shoulder-length, with a trim figure, about 22 years old. We had a pleasant visit and talked about the possibility of getting a theatre going. She was very enthusiastic. The next few days were spent mentioning the idea to others, and reporting to one another for moral support. She talked to some of the Coast Guard wives and a number of them seemed interested.

I took the big step and went to the Navy Special Services Officer – Lieutenant Adrian B. Morris, Jr. – "Sonny."

Sonny is a southern boy; he's been out here almost two years. He does not get things done at a rapid pace. At our first meeting, however, things went fine. He told me a theatre had been tried, but there had been no one to keep the group together. He showed me a Quonset hut across the street from his office – bldg 6-18 – that had a low platform at one end of it. That, eventually, became our theatre.

Commander McCaffery suggested that I see the Executive Officer of the station, Lieutenant Commander Laing, noted for his tight fist and lack of humor. It was a good suggestion. He was friendly enough, but tried to find reasons why it wouldn't work. He wanted some by-laws in writing -- where, who, how, etc. As he said, he was supposed to throw a wet blanket on things, so if they were merely flashes, they would die before they started. I went back to Morris; he called the Exec and assured him that there would be no immediate outlay of money. That seemed to pacify the Exec and we went on our way.

It took a while for me to understand that people like Lieutenant Morris and Lieutenant Commander Laing were simply doing what was expect of them, that they were following a routine that worked for them, and exceptions to that were welcomed slowly and cautiously, especially if they would disrupt that routine.

And cause more work.

In retrospect the notion of "putting on a play," at that time and in that place, had a fanciful "Hollywood" element, like the movies where Mickey Rooney and Judy Garland and a bunch of kids exclaim "Hey – why don't we put on a show? My uncle's got a barn – " and they end up putting on a musical that matches Broadway.

Nothing like that would be our outcome, I knew, but the process would be the same: you have to decide what you're going to put on, hold auditions to get actors to play the roles, have a "stage" suitable for the show with lights and maybe a curtain, work out a rehearsal schedule that suits most of the actors and accommodates those who have conflicts, find a place for rehearsals if the stage isn't available, get people to work backstage to help you design and build scenery and paint it, gather furniture and props and costumes the actors need, prepare and distribute publicity so that you have an audience to see what you accomplished doing all the previous things.

In our situation, most of those jobs would fall to me. I had been involved in "shows" since I took tap-dancing lessons at the age of four, and most of my experience had been as a performer, but during those stints I saw all the other jobs being done, and in some situations I got involved doing them, like painting scenery and setting lights. In high school I had written and directed scenes for student shows, and with a minor in theatre in college came courses in acting and directing, as well as exposure to the non-acting jobs during our main-stage productions.

So to get our theatre off the ground, I would have to be a producer – procure or provide the stage, the actors, all the physical and personnel needs, as well as manage publicity; a director – audition the actors and get them to perform their roles so the show has the impact you envision, plan and carry out the lighting and scenery; and possibly be an actor – if there was an empty spot in the cast.

I talked with some of the people Jan had contacted. One had four kids and number five was on the way. But word was spreading, and there was hope. Jan, Paul, and a score of others suggested that I be sure to have something concrete to put in the hands of any comers at a first meeting. Interest wanes easily out here, they warned. So I had two scenes mimeographed, and a little bit of propaganda to give encouragement and explain what I had in mind. Most of the stencil-cutting I had to do myself. Already Sonny was slowing down.

The notice about the theatre was put in the Plan of the Day, and at the first meeting on August 26 we had about ten people. We read scripts and I talked to them and got some idea of what kind of talent we had. An Australian named Lloyd George auditioned – tall, 34 years old, with a black mustache and experience in the theatre – and he fell nicely into two roles. Jan fit nicely, too. But that was about it.

27 August 1953
Dear Mom,

Received your letter yesterday. Was most glad to get. I had a small accident with my typewriter [I think I dropped it!] *so while it is being repaired, I'll have to pen my way home.*

I've been keeping myself pretty busy or I would write more often. We haven't started standing watches yet, although I wish we would – we'd have more time off then. But several things are happening right now. The C.G. appropriations have been cut, so they are thinking of closing up the Rescue Center out here or turning it over to the Navy. The Navy, however, is very pleased with the job the Coast Guard has been doing, and wants us to stay. The Coast Guard Commander doesn't want any slip-ups right now especially, so he's reluctant to give us a free hand.

But the guys we are relieving are due to go in a week or so. They want us to take over as soon as possible. The two forces don't see eye to eye. At any rate, soon we'll be on watches – we'll have to when they go.

. . . Today I took a sight-seeing trip around the island by plane. A Navy flier connected with our office was putting in flight time, so he took me along. Quite a beautiful place – very green, and hilly in most parts. Some big cliffs along the shore, as well as some nice beaches. A lot of native villages around, which someday I shall visit.

. . . We had a typhoon scare yesterday, but it passed over. Been pretty hot lately, too, and gad, the mosquitoes. Really awful.

Finally we took over the watches, Sarge and I. The commander was a little uncertain about our abilities. He had just been informed that these outlying rescue centers were under fire in Washington as being duplication and therefore expensive; he wanted no slip-ups now. But as time rolled on, our place in the center rolled toward us. Chuck and Mo left, and we had to carry the ball. Up to the time of writing this – three weeks since starting to stand watches – not a single incident has occurred.

A little over one week on a new duty station and you hear rumors that the place, and your job, might be eliminated. Maybe that news should be good for morale, if you think you might get a better deal, but it throws a heavy dose of uncertainty on everything which can lead to lack of commitment for the job you have to do now.

The armistice that stopped the fighting had been signed in July, so automatically the idea of budget cuts kicked in and everything "non-essential" would soon go. But what exactly would be non-essential, and how soon was "soon?" The rumor mill could be general or specific, and often contradictory.

You learn from the older, more experienced guys that rumors are part of military life; someone has always gotten some "scoop" from someone else and spreads the word that things might be changing. You want to plan ahead? — it makes it difficult. But you realize that it will take considerable time for any big and permanent changes to be made. So you learn to shrug and keep going.

And that's what happened with the theatre. A few nights later we had a second meeting.

The second meeting produced a few more interested personnel, among then the Exec's wife. The Exec himself came. I had seen them at dinner in the mess, all dressed up. My mouth dropped when I saw them come into our dirty Quonset; I was also quite pleased. It's like having a bird in the hand.

I had decided to do scenes from several shows; that way I could see what kind of talent we had and also see what play would best suit our facilities. The scenes were from 'Mister Roberts,' 'The Man Who Came to Dinner,' and 'The Moon Is Blue.'

'Mister Roberts' was a natural – all men and about the Navy; no costume problems and the actors could identify with their roles. 'The Moon Is Blue' required only two actors and an easily suggested locale – the observation tower of the Empire State Building. 'The Man Who Came to Dinner' included a number of women who were the majority of my talent. Also, my high school had put on 'The Man' (an all-male version which amazingly played very well) and I had played the leading role of Sheridan Whiteside, so I knew the play well and knew it was a crowd-pleaser.

At the second meeting scripts for all scenes were passed out and the roles cast with the people we had. Those players said they would try to get others. There would be another scheduled audition, but anyone was welcome to come to a rehearsal and I would audition them then.

Our theatre, Quonset 6-18, was 20 feet wide, so its semi-circular structure gave us a maximum height of 10 feet. The platform across the end was about a foot high and maybe 10 feet deep. Since the curving walls took away about 3 or 4 feet of usable space on each side, we had a performing area 14 feet wide maximum – less if the actor was tall.

A couple of Chiefs from the VS-25 Squadron came to the rescue in getting people and in dressing up the stage. Chief Harry Morris (not Sonny) was a life saver. He "boon docked" (stole or permanently borrowed) various target materials and made curtains for the front. Lloyd George and I made tabs for the sides. Pretty soon we had curtains we hadn't used yet.

The plan was to rehearse for the next three weeks and perform The Scenes on September 20. Enthusiasm was high with all participants; this was something different, a break in their routine, a filler for those large "what do I do now?" periods that weighed on everyone. And a chance to socialize and meet different people. I was standing watches by this time and had time to spare. My theatre instincts kicked in and soon we were working hard and doing 'the best we could.' If it didn't work out, there was nothing lost.

One Sunday afternoon, I was waiting in the theatre for people to try out. Only one showed, a woman named Gladys whom Chief Morris had talked to. She's a chief's wife, a position next to God. Her face looked rather worn and she was very thin and had crooked teeth. About 35, I thought. And an old looking one at that. I could smell alcohol on her breath. It was 1:30 in the afternoon.

During the half hour we talked and read lines, I learned that she has only one lung, doesn't drive because of it, was a USO entertainer, also on radio, and had seen so many people die that she wants to be something besides "just a mother."

I gave her the part of Harriet, in 'The Man Who Came to Dinner' – the idiot sister.

She had three lines, but she really rehearsed them. Her husband read the cues for her, and over and over them she went. She was doing fairly well – a little hard to direct, perhaps (always an explanation of why she hadn't done it a certain way), but at least she was there. I soon learned that her husband hoped the theatre might have a therapeutic effect on her, keep her away from the bottle. They have three children, the youngest only a few months old.

She showed up one night with her hair down to the middle of her back. "Perfect," I thought. But how do you tell someone she looks like an idiot and make them feel flattered? Pictures were to be taken at the next rehearsal, and in the course of the conversation, Chief Amador said, "I like your hair that way." So she wore it that way.

From Ray Davis I learned that on the Saturday night following, she had been caught up a palm tree in her high heels kicking down the coconuts. I also learned that her previous experience had been gained at a burlesque house in Brooklyn. During the next week she informed me that she was going back to the states in about a month on a medical, but she'd be here for our production. Apparently the husband figured she was getting out of hand.

The next Saturday night proved him right. She was drunk again and this time hurled a beer mug at him. It missed, crashed and broke, and hit their baby causing lacerations on the face and shoulder. The very next night she tried to kill herself by slashing her left wrist. She had called the dispensary and asked how to commit suicide by slashing your wrists. The seaman on duty probably told her to sleep it off. Later she called for an ambulance – she had cut her left wrist with a razor.

Ray Davis was duty officer and he was called in. Everybody was being mean to her, he said, so he tried to be nice. She was so grateful that when she left for the Naval Hospital psycho ward, she took both his hands and thanked him.

He told me she had tried to prove her sanity by saying, "I'm in the little theatre, and Ensign Connolly just complimented me on my acting." The doctors just looked at one another. What else?

Chapter Nine

Slow Bell or No Bell

14 Sept
Dear Mom and all –
Happy Birthday from me to me. Thank you for the cards.
. . . This place is slow death. Around and around the clock goes – and that's just about how existence is here. Right now my mood isn't the best. Things aren't going exceptionally well with the shows. It's about time, though. Things had been too smooth of late. After these scenes get put on, I'll probably do "The Moon Is Blue" which requires only four people. Around here people lose interest so damn quickly – we've been lucky in that only two or three have dropped out. But watch schedules and night flights etc. keep others from one rehearsal or another. If ever I get everybody there for rehearsal I'll be glad.

Don at Japanese WWII gun emplacement

Spare time on this island holds the real story, if there is one. There are plenty of people out here, mostly men. There is plenty of liquor. As a result, the men mostly drink. They also sleep. They go to the movies, too. They read. But that about covers the activities of the majority of the people here. It doesn't take long for Guam Fever to attack. Its symptoms are a lack of motion brought about by a lack of energy. It finds its victims in all ages and sexes. It develops quickly and its torment can be soothed only by passive pleasures. Its mental effect is that of the one track mind: "when am I going back to the States?" the patient continually screams. That becomes his one obsession – he thinks it as he drinks, he thinks it as he watches the movies, even as he reads Mickey Spillane. Its only cure is a return to the Big Island, the land of the Tall Quonsets. Then, however, the shock from the sudden change may be fatal.

Not everyone falls before it. There is usually some sort of activity somewhere. But try to sustain any interest in anything, and you find yourself all alone. That at least is what I was told. Let's hope it depends on the individual.

However, it didn't take long for my deep funk, the first symptoms of Guam Fever, to level out.

20 Sept 1953
Dear Trio –
Yep, it's time for another long one again. Seems as if the last one got quick and lengthy response from all of you.
. . . My "island paradise" as Bob calls it has turned out to be a rather pleasant place. No paradise, however, but on the other hand, no place of torment, either. We're on duty hours now and have spare time aplenty. There hasn't been one incident since I started standing watches; if we don't have one soon, I'll forget what to do.
Mom asked to know just what my job is. The Coast Guard is responsible for safety at sea. This means everybody at sea, or for that matter, in the air or on the land related to the sea. But principally at sea. Out here we have our own planes and ships which do most of the rescuing. Whenever we receive word that someone is in distress, we inform the units that can carry out the rescue and they go to work. Sometimes we have to use Navy or Air Force facilities for a big job, and that's where the coordinating comes in. So you can see in a way we are a lot like firemen, just sitting and waiting for something to happen. When something does happen you have to know what facilities are available at the various places. The big CG ships get rotated every three weeks; in order to give them something to do while here, and to try out

various methods of searching, we have drills.

Commander McCaffery has developed a search pattern that's an improvement over the ones previously used; it employs radar to keep track of the planes that are searching. That way we can see when they aren't keeping in the predetermined search track, and tell them how far off they are. They correct that amount and all the area gets searched. It's very easy to leave large gaps in the ocean when searching by plane; and a raft isn't very easy to spot from a plane.

His search consists of two planes flying in legs that cross at right angles to each other – forming a checkerboard. It has advantages that I won't go into, compared to the old method of one following the other or flying parallel. The main thing about the drills is that something positive is being done about Search and Rescue. In the past nobody has been scientific in approach; at least some thinking is being done. It's part of my job to help prepare these drills, and at times to go aboard the ship partaking and observe. After a while, I'll probably be in charge of the drill aboard and help the ship carry it out.

Every officer in the service has what are called collateral duties. I think Jim was education officer and fire marshal. My jobs – I have two – are not nearly so glamorous. I'm logistics officer (paper, pencils, paper clips) and (gad!) statistics officer. Luckily the latter is merely a glorified file clerk. I make out reports of incidents, tabulate them (not difficult with our activity) and in general keep track of pertinent and impertinent info. Most of it is the latter. Anyway, it gives me something to do while on watch, and to look busy while the commander is around.

While I've mentioned the commander – he is really a swell guy. Named McCaffery, a Catholic (happy, Gene?), all girls (happy, Don?), the oldest is about 12. (No!!) As we sailors say, he takes everything on a slow bell. As yet he has nothing to chew me out about. I hope I don't give him the opportunity. Actually it isn't necessary to make an attempt to look busy or impress him; but since he is the way he is, I always feel that I ought to be doing something to earn my keep. If he were a stinker, I wouldn't do a thing.

By September 20th I had been to sea twice on training drills, both with Commander McCaffery on the CGC Finch, a cutter out of San Francisco. The first time I only observed. The second time would have been the same except that the captain of the Finch, another slow-bell guy like McCaffery, suggested I take over the deck for a while, which meant I would be the operator, the one in charge of what's happening on the ship. So for about three hours I gave orders to the helmsman (orders someone else gave to me), made log entries, figured out various weather information, and granted permissions to a myriad of sailors to do their duties, saluting each and every time – more salutes were given in 30 minutes than in the previous 3 months. For several long stretches I was alone on the bridge and was quite impressed with my authority over some 300-plus feet of ship.

One time when I was alone, a sailor came on the bridge to do something or other. Another followed him shortly, and looking around the deck, saw only me. He turned to the first guy who just seemed to be hanging around and said, "Who's got the deck?" The first guy said, "Beats me." So the second guy figured out since I was the only officer *on* the deck, I must be officer *of* the deck. He came over to me, saluted, and asked permission to relieve the lookout. I saluted, granted permission, and he climbed the ladder and was out of sight.

A minute later the old lookout climbed down from his perch and came onto the bridge. He, too, saw only me. He looked up at the guy who had just relieved him and said, "Who's got the deck?" It was becoming a refrain. The new lookout indicated me, so the old lookout came over. He saluted and, as appropriate, held the salute as he started his report: "Sir, I have been properly relieved as lookout – "

Thinking that was the end of his report, I returned the salute. But he continued: " – and request permission to lay below – "

The ship was rolling to starboard and he and I, both still holding the salute, leaned in unison to port.

" – to relieve the helm –"

The roll eased to an end and started the other direction; we slowly changed our sway to compensate, but our salutes never faltered.

" – steering course zero-nine-zero."

That was it. The ship had made two full, lazy rolls, with

both of us, hands at our foreheads, waists bending back and forth in slow motion, maintaining military decorum, he talking the whole time.

It struck me funny and I had to keep from laughing. I probably looked just as funny to him.

One thing my shipboard experience taught me – I was glad I was on land, be it ever so small. It's nice to be able to look at a different face once in a while.

In a few weeks my life on Guam had fallen into three pretty discreet sections – my work or Coast Guard world, my little theatre world, and my personal world— letters, books, church, the German course, the gym, the beach, and people

Sarge turned out to be a very compatible partner who wound up sharing in much of all of those worlds. Besides working together – at least relieving each other periodically – and sharing living quarters in "The Castle," he got into the theatre activities and helped in any way he could, building and lugging anything needed, working with the stage crew, even acting, which he had never done.

My "hurry-up-and-get-it-done" approach to most every activity took a lesson from Sarge's steady pace and soft laugh that worked for him in most situations. Seeing how he reacted and interacted made me realize that he used those mannerisms to cover a soft self-confidence and a cautious mind-set that he wanted to break out of, or at least peel back, and in the process they allowed him to be part of things without making foolish commitments. There never seemed to be any peaks of emotion; in fact, not much emotion at all. He seemed to acknowledge accomplishments and disappointments with the same soft laugh.

Through Sarge I had met Ray Davis, and Ray soon was drawn into our lives. Like Sarge, he got involved in the burgeoning theatre and responded to my need for actors; the base newspaper lists him in the cast of "Mister Roberts." I don't recall which part he played.

He had been on the island for some months, maybe a year, and had become involved in some extra-curricular activities – the base football team and a course in American literature at the

Guam Territorial College, an extension of Ohio State. Classes were held a short drive away at Navy headquarters (CincPac-Marianas) – a set of buildings on a hill in the center of the island, waggishly called "The Top o' the Mar". Sarge and I eventually sat in on a couple of the classes – Faulkner was the topic – after which we went to dinner at the up-scale officer's club suitable for the higher brass. Besides Faulkner, Ray was interested in the teacher, early 30s, bright and self-confident, who joined us for dinner. They began dating.

Ray is tall and inclined to be heavy; he's always going on a diet, but offer him a cookie and he can't refuse; the same with beer. He comes from a fairly well-to-do family, as evidenced how fast and casually he drives his car and how he fails to pick up behind himself. Good-natured enough, and not a boor or a bore, but so definitely patterned that he might have been bred on tea and beans. He helps coach the football team, but as Sarge (who is the team's equipment manager) says, he never really does anything, just stands around and watches most of the time. He's in the Third Battalion, a group of "island defenders" who train every Saturday morning in the boondocks. That of course is not of his own volition.

Ray eventually moved into our hut. We three ensigns could not have presented more different images: Sarge with his go-along attitude, make-no-fuss demeanor; I looking for something meaningful to fill the time and naively assuming that others would agree or at least be supportive; and Ray exuding entitlement with words or body language, letting you know that he'd rather be in the northeast U.S. associated with people who share his Ivy League connections and the privilege that ensued. He was from Chicago and had found it stifling; my being from St. Louis and attending a Catholic university there received raised eyebrows. Harvard had led him to shed the chains of both the Midwest and the Catholic Church.

Through Ray, Sarge and I met the Krechs—Lieutenant (junior grade) Shepard Krech, Jr., a medical doctor, his wife, Nora, and their two pre-teen children, Amy and Little Shep. Ray knew Shep from the BOQ, Shep's living quarters until his family arrived, at which time they set up in a civilian house near Tumon Beach – military housing wasn't yet available. On Labor Day they put a picnic together, invited Ray, and he invited us, and Sarge invited an attractive Wellesley student named Dee O'Connor.

Shep and Nora were in their mid-30s, intelligent, friendly and witty, from New York City, but planning to move to the Eastern Shore of Maryland where Shep could have an unhurried medical practice and enjoy his beloved duck hunting.

It was refreshing to be with the Krechs. They welcomed us openly and provided an up-scale picnic at Tarague Beach with some off-beat food and drink. It was obvious they enjoyed younger, college-educated people and the banter and laughter that came with them.

Shep's entrance into the Navy was recent. He was a reserve. His medical training had been in a government-sponsored program during World War II and he had not served any military time when the war ended. His name was on the call-up rolls when the Korean War started, and he was still young and healthy enough for active duty. His call-up had been a surprise and meant putting on hold plans for moving and for the kids' schooling. In her short time as an officer's wife, Nora had avoided the usual and expected relationships with the other wives. She had a lot of time to entertain the likes of us.

At the picnic on Labor Day, we played football on the beach and Shep twisted his leg and activated his varicose veins. It was a mess – Ray and Nora took him home, and Amy and Little Shep stayed with Sarge, Dee and me. They were very composed. Amy (about 12) served the food and saw that everyone had enough.

That was the beginning with the Krechs. We went again to Tarague Beach the next Sunday and a couple of times since. They are wonderful people – rather well to-do, but you wouldn't know it, except that they are cultured but not in the least stuffy. They talk French a lot with Sarge and everybody gets a big kick out of it. Nora apparently has never really had to "housewife" but she does well enough.

At beach, Tumon Bay, Agana, Guam. Sarge Horwood and the Krechs – Little Shep, Amy, Nora and Shep

They became our oasis (if that's possible on a tropical island), our energizer when Guam Fever threatened, our sympathetic but non-intruding ears.

Chapter Ten

Up and Running

NAS Little Theater Workshop Plays Tomorrow Night

After many weeks of extensive rehearsals and with the cooperation of Lt A.B. Morris, Special Services Officer, the Little Theater Players will make their debut tomorrow evening at the NAS Little Theater, located in Hut 6-18, just back of the cobbler shop.

We were now the Little Theater Players, with capital letters. The base paper declared it publicly, with dates for performances (September 26 and 27) and cast and director announced for all to see. Certainly there was no turning back now, although a few weeks before there were brief thoughts of throwing in the towel. I had been warned about the lethargy, hovering like the rain clouds, but Ensign Blue-Eye would not be dimmed.

[From letter of Sept 20, 1953]
To make a long story short, we are presenting three scenes – one scene from "Moon Is Blue," and "The Man Who Came to Dinner" and two scenes from "Mister Roberts." Our number has grown to about 20 or 25; several have come and gone, which is to be expected. That's especially true among the enlisted men here. They lose interest so darn easily; for a while I was really disgusted. "Mr. Roberts" requires about 10 men for the scenes we're doing; it was really a chore getting them. Some of the talent is very good. We've got one Australian (a civilian

worker) who is terrific – plays "The Man" to a tee. Also does "Doc" in "Mister Roberts," despite his accent. A Coast Guard wife is very good, too. There are a couple of type-castings who wouldn't be much good in anything else.

One woman has improved a lot since rehearsals began. I was afraid to use her at first, although she was very interested; after I heard her read it seemed hopeless, but she is pretty good now. She happens to be Phyllis Laing, the Executive Officer's wife – a nice addition to any organization. She is a wonderful person, and I'm glad things are working out as they are.

The Australian, Lloyd George, worked for QANTAS, the Australian airline, as a coordinator or representative for the planes going to or coming from Korea with Australian troops. The planes refueled on Guam and usually remained overnight . Lloyd met the planes and handled the logistics for plane and people. He had an associate, Bob, a mechanic who serviced the planes when needed. His own schedule, as a result, was pretty open, and he gave me a lot of help with chores and encouragement.

But he was not immune to Guam Fever. He had big roles in two scenes which was more commitment than he had made in a long time. He felt that there were too many rehearsals, and maybe so, but with only four weeks to get everything done, and the ups and downs of attendance at rehearsal, I wanted to be on the safe side.

It's interesting in retrospect that the men were more likely to miss rehearsals than the women. Maybe the men felt there was enough scheduling in their lives, and getting moving after a work day was too much to ask. Of course, it was the men who had the changeable hours which led to conflicts with rehearsal. Many of the officers were married and had family responsibilities even if there were no children. Whatever the reason it was frustrating; one day you took a step forward, and the next day you did back flips trying to keep everything from falling apart. Dick Hollands who played the Mister Roberts role didn't show up for an afternoon rehearsal on a weekend, scheduled because everyone said they could make it. At the next rehearsal I told him how it messed up the other actors, and he said that his wife had wanted to go to the beach, so they did.

The two actors in 'The Moon Is Blue' were Jan Yost and a tall, self-confident enlisted man named Mike Harrison. The scene became a lesson for me in discretion and human relations.

There was a crisis when I informed an enlisted man that Jan thought we had better tone down the kissing in their scene because this is Guam and she's an officer's wife, etc. She realizes now that it was a silly fear, as I should have realized then. Harrison was hurt, and quit. Of course, naïve me, I didn't get the reason for it. Then another guy quit out of friendship. Finally I got things straightened out – or they straightened themselves.

I just got him to come back to rehearsal to see what could be done; no one said anything about it. Jan and he talked about things, then started going over the lines. The first times we did it we left out the kissing. Then about a week ago they asked me to rehearse them in the afternoon, so they could work on their lines. During the rehearsal the time seemed right to take the bull by the horns, so I said, "All right, while we're here, let's put in the business." All three of us blushed. The first attempts were rather furtive, but now they kiss at every re-hearsal and it looks good.

28 September 1953
Dear Mom and all –
A bit of good news. The plays came off Sat and Sun night, and were a big success. Yes, I was quite despondent for a while; a lot of enlisted men would come and go, and watch schedules kept some from coming, and all the stage equipment had to be scrounged from somewhere.

I was especially worried about the lighting, which we had none of, and not much outlook for getting any. The Special Services officer, who would be in charge of procuring same, is not much good. Also, things are pretty hard to get on the island, especially electrical equipment. That may seem strange for a military installation, but it's true. Well, luckily there were some enlisted men who had some idea of what was needed, and equipment was gotten somewhere and somehow, and we had light. Had a dimmer, too, so we could lower and raise the lights.

The first night most of the brass were there. I introduced each of the scenes. "Mister Roberts" was especially well received – the guys playing the enlisted men were much better than they or I had expected. Most of them were inexperienced, and one big problem was getting them to wait for laughs and timing their lines correctly. But even the first night they were good. I told them to have fun with their parts, and they did.

Two friends, Nick Santiago and Bob Murphy from the same squadron as Chief Morris, were very dependable about rehearsals and worked on their lines. Probably the chief, in his pleasant but firm way, made sure they showed up. They really came through. Murphy had never been on stage before and he delighted in every laugh he got. He's a short, well-built Irishman who's always smiling; Nick is slight, tightly-built, of Latin descent. They are crew partners.

"The Moon Is Blue" was good too. I would have preferred a different actor, but it went over well, and that's all I was concerned about. "The Man Who Came to Dinner" was liked too, but it wasn't as hilarious as "Mister Roberts" mainly because it's a lot more sophisticated.

By the way, Gladys, the chief's wife, was in the play, as Harriet, as originally cast. The role was empty for a while – maybe my fingers were crossed that someone would drop from the sky. With just three lines, the part could be cut. But she was not kept at the hospital after being held for observation for slashing her wrists, so she came to rehearsal. My mouth almost hit the floor when she walked in. And she did okay in the show.

After the first performance of The Scenes, a group of us – Sarge, Ray, his teacher, Lorraine, and I went to the officers' club at the Top O' the Mar to celebrate. We had had a few drinks first with Lloyd at our own officers' club so we were feeling good when we arrived. Lorraine put down numerous shots of scotch and seemed perfectly sober. At least she was laughing at me! Sarge and I were dancing alone in the patio and cutting a mean rug. Ray and I did the Charleston, too. Lorraine and I did a Mexican Hat Dance, and all in all, I was really living it up. It was the closest thing to being looped I've ever come.

I hope to do "The Man Who" sometime before Christmas. Enthusiasm for the scenes was great and that might help us get some place better. I thank you for all the prayers which I know helped (I did quite a bit of praying myself). You can now direct them toward finding some place suitable for big productions.

This is it for now. I've got a lot of letters to write, I've been neglecting them because of the play. Love to all.

Even with its large cast, "The Man Who Came to Dinner" seemed the best choice for our first full production for the same reasons for doing a scene: Good women's roles, a very strong actor for the leading role, my familiarity with it, and comedy that's almost actor-proof. Also, it takes place in a wintery Christmas setting which would be good for morale and appropriate to a December presentation.

We had enthusiasm. And a plan. Now all we needed was a stage big enough and equipped to do a full production. And more actors.

But everything hinged on the stage.

People aware of the Navy way of doing things said I had to write to the Navy captain to get the necessary permissions and financing. The Special Services Officer, Lieutenant Morris, helped me write the letter in the official format. As for money, he said, "Oh, ask for $500, just to get us started."

The letter was written with my signature and sent by Lieutenant Morris through the chain of command. He said we'd just have to sit back and wait.

Okay. A rest would do me good, a much needed recharge for the battery, although not so long that our enthusiasm would flag and old habits return.

Just a stage, sir – well, a pretty big stage, if you don't mind, sir.

Somehow – somewhere –

Chapter Eleven

Rest and Respite

We had a picnic for the Little Theatre. Just about everybody was there, including the Exec, Lieutenant Commander Laing, who came with his wife. And Gladys and husband and family were there.

We had a wonderful time – I went "reef swimming" [snorkeling, as it's called now] for the first time. Used fins and a mask and went out to where the reef dips a little and the water is 15 feet at the deepest. The tide has cut a lot of channels in the coral, and some of them are fairly deep. The top of the reef is sharp with coral, but the channels near the bottom are worn smooth and can be swum through without scratching yourself. With the masks you can see the fish – some of them are exquisite. All sorts of colors and shapes and sizes. Like you see on tavern walls or in rathskellers, and never believe they exist. Well, now I know they do.

We swam for an hour or so and then had grilled hamburgers and beer and soda. Some of us stayed after the married folk had left – Lloyd, Nick, Murphy, Thomas, Chief Morris. We did acrobatics on the beach and just messed around in general.

Little Theatre beach party after The Scenes

In my scrapbook are pictures of the picnic. One is of Lieutenant Commander Laing in matching swimsuit and shirt, sitting relaxed in the shade, reading. Another is some of the ladies in the show. And some of the troops. Great memories.

Ray Davis and I have been going to visit the Krechs to play bridge. Nora can't stand "Navy wives" mainly because she says all they talk about is housework and the Navy. Nora and Shep say they enjoy us fellows and sure seem to, so we keep going back.

One night in early October when Ray and I were down there playing bridge, a message came that Nora's father had died. He had cancer and they expected to get word like that, but not so soon. She was disturbed and cried, but realizing that not much could be done, we went on playing bridge for a bit. Took her mind off a little, I guess.

About 11:30 we left, and Ray was feeling tired and logy (the Scotch, you know) and asked me to drive. I was backing out the long road leading to their house and put the car in the ditch on the side. Guam roads aren't very good, and I'm not used to Ray's car, and I had had something to drink, too. Because of the death we didn't want to disturb the Krechs and ask them to drive us to the air station so we just left the car and started walking. The air station was in sight in the distance, but up a very steep and wooded cliff. The other way around was several miles. So Ray, being in the Third Battalion that does a lot of climbing around in the jungle on Saturdays, said, "Let's cut across the boondocks, there are plenty of paths."

We did. But we didn't find any paths. We started up the hill at a likely place, only to find that this hill dropped off to nothing, and the real cliff was ahead, still to be negotiated. It was pitch black; Ray led the way and I followed. We stumbled over all sorts of refuse, logs, etc. Ray finally just disappeared into a small ravine. He had no way to come back up, so I had to follow him which was accomplished by grabbing the nearest bush and dropping into oblivion. I tore my shirt and got a head full of dirt as I slid down the hillside. We tried the cliff itself, but after a landslide or two, we gave up the idea. Instead we followed a path along a pipeline that leads into the base. It came out at the far end of the base. About 1:30 a.m. we were trudging down the main drag of the air station, tired, dirty and somewhat amused. A torn shirt and dirty pants and some tired muscles the next day were the only casualties.

Amazingly Ray seemed undisturbed by any of the trials – just kept on walking, even to the extent of dropping out of sight. Looking back it was a lot of fun. But next time I won't rely on Ray, I'll call the Coast Guard to come and get me!

15 October 1953
Dear Mom and all,

It's raining like hell here. Has been since 10 pm last night and now it is 3 pm. There were winds up to about 50 miles per hour this morning. The rain blows against the louvered sides of the hut and sprays all over the beds. This is like it was when I arrived. There are no glass windows, so in the front where there is screen and no louvers, the rain comes in at will. But up to this time the weather has been fine. So can't really complain.

The second check book arrived and the pictures. It was good to see the old homestead again. Also the family's bright faces. Mom, don't ever wear that hat you have on in the picture with Gram in front of the house. Throw it away. . . .

About Christmas for me. I'm thinking of buying myself a bicycle out here. Can get good foreign ones pretty cheap. Why don't you folks chip in whatever you want and put in my account?

Please send as soon as possible, 1) my raincoat – olive colored, very light 2) my two pairs of cord (seersucker) trousers and 3) my long play record albums: Carousel, Guys and Dolls, King and I (45 rpm) A Tree Grows in Brooklyn, and Streetcar Named Desire. I think those are the only ones I have. If it costs too much to send all that by airmail, send it regular. Airmail Parcel Post, I mean. The other packages took 40 days.

Things have been uneventful here. Been taking it easy after the other plays. Am just about ready to launch "The Man Who Came to Dinner." As yet we have received no verification on our request for money or for a place to put the plays on. Without money and space we can't do a thing. . . .

My German is progressing. Auf wiedersehen.
Love, Don

As someone who enjoys warm weather and swimming and at least the idea of things tropical, I found my day-to-day personal world, when the rain didn't tie you down, quite enjoyable. Duty watches and Little Theatre aside, there was plenty of time for the beach, reading, letter writing (probably I had overdone the call to relatives and friends to keep in touch and save me from boredom) and being with people I had come to enjoy.

When you felt you were getting into a rut with the daily routine, if you found yourself counting the days till your return to the land of the Tall Quonsets, you could help lift your spirits by enjoying the beauties and attractions of the Island. Guam has been called one of the most beautiful islands in the Pacific. And it is very beautiful with a rugged terrain and green growth and tropical breezes under billowing clouds in a startling blue sky. But then – it was always green, even when the seasons are supposed to change; the sky's brilliant blue was often gray with rain and rain clouds; the breezes sometimes grew to typhoon strength that could knock you over. You had to learn to enjoy it while you could.

The best time of day around here is sunset. The working day is over and the night of play is about to begin. The heat has melted away, and if the sky is clear the stage is set for a cool, lovely, enjoyable evening. The curtain raiser on this pleasant scene is the sunset. There is always a ring of clouds around the island – Guam is reputed to have the most beautiful cloud formations in the world, we're close to the equatorial front. If everything is right, the setting sun paints these clouds in wonderful shades of yellow, orange, red, and even purple. On both beach parties we had with the gang from the Little Theatre the sunsets were spectacular. The ocean reflects the cloud colors and the whole display takes on a multi-dimensional quality. From our hut it's beautiful, too – palm trees silhouetted in the foreground with all that color blazing, then burning slowly away. It's the South Seas you read about in books. It's the best picker-upper I know.

The most beautiful spot I've seen so far is Tarague beach, at the north end of the island. It's below some sheer cliffs that are covered with foliage. The road leading down was blasted from the cliff. The first view is through the gorge made in the cliff before the road winds down the side. The beach is covered with white sand, and has plenty of palm trees for shade. Unfortunately the swimming is rather poor, except when the tide is high. But then the lifeguards are so watchful you can hardly get any distance from shore.

The Little Theatre had led to connections with a number of people, especially civilians, officer's wives, and enlisted men.

We had become a community, loose but caring, now with a bond that set us a bit apart from those non-theatre others. At the officers' club those Others probably got tired of hearing Us rehash our two-night triumph. If they did, there was plenty of booze and laughter and singing to help drown us out.

If they weren't going to the outdoor movie or the USO entertainment that came through periodically, it was usual for the men and couples to go to their clubs – the enlisted had a club, too – on weekend nights and sometimes during the week. There was always music from a juke box for singing and dancing, card games (especially Acey-Ducey) and opportunity for conversation and kibitzing.

On one of my first visits to the O'Club, sitting at the bar drinking a Tom Collins (the popular gin drink of the time), I was asked by a navy flyer next to me if I had brought my skis – "yeah, there's snow on Mt. Lam-lam. Haven't you seen it?" Of course there wasn't; Mt. Lam-lam was the highest point on the island, about 1300 feet, trees and jungle to the top.

Friday at the O'Club was Fight Night – from 6:00 to 7:15 p.m. the drinks were ten cents. The tenor of the evening resulting from such availability is the source of the name. As yet I've only witnessed loud singing, wild dancing and some drunken antics, but no fights. Frankly, I'm disappointed.

There wasn't much drinking at home when I was growing up. The country had just abolished Prohibition in 1933 and a lot of people like my parents and grandparents who might have had alcoholic drinks had not started or re-established the habit. Also, the 1930's was Depression-time, and alcoholic drinks were expensive. Pepsi-Cola was the "fun drink" in our house. Then came World War II with its restrictions, and drinking never entered the picture.

However, on a back shelf in our pantry at home there was a bottle of whiskey that came out when we had a special guest. We knew the habits of our relatives and maybe on special occasions they would have beer or wine. The whiskey was for other guests, like one of the parish priests. My mother would say,

"Father, would you like a high-ball?" Usually he would, and out came the whiskey (that's all we called it, not bourbon, which it probably was, or rye or scotch) and the sweet lemon-lime carbonated soda 7-Up. To me, a high-ball – whiskey and 7-Up – was how you drank hard liquor.

In college, I never became a beer drinker like some of the guys. After a play rehearsal when some of the older fellows (many were ex-GIs) would go to a bar for beer, I would get a bus home to the suburbs to get up early the next day for class. Besides, it was expensive and I was always watching my weight.

In my junior year, I went with a friend from high school now in college with me to visit high school friends who were attending Notre Dame University. We took the train and wound up in the club car. Dressed in suits (as almost everyone did then when traveling) we looked old enough to drink and my friend asked for "a bourbon and branch water." I asked for the same, not knowing what to expect. It was, probably, my first sophisticated drink, at least by name.

In the O'Club on Guam it was very easy to sit at the bar, get into a conversation and down one drink after another. By that time I had learned to drink Tom Collins – gin in a carbonated lemony mix; the recipe says it has lemon juice and refined sugar or syrup, but I recall it having a tart taste, not sweet like lemonade. In that humid, tropical climate it seemed the perfect "light" drink. However, enough of them took their toll with a "bit of a head" the next day. That was not the desired outcome, but the camaraderie at the club was enjoyable so I arranged with the bartender to order a Don Collins, and he would give me the straight Collins mix with all the decorative fruit.

Another reality of military life is making and losing friends. Maybe you can't really call them friends, the time together is so short. But when it has been meaningful, you miss them like friends. That's what struck me about the story of "Mister Roberts" – a guy does things to help others, to make their life easier, and when he leaves and gets killed, they finally appreciate what he did for them.

That was my feeling about the guys who had worked on

The Scenes with me, especially those from the VS-25 squadron – Nick, Murphy, Chief Morris and Chief Amador and a number of others – who not only acted but built scenery and scrounged lighting equipment. We soon heard that their squadron would be leaving in early November.

So I arranged another beach party, just for the fellows. About twelve of us went, roasted hot dogs – Lloyd had never eaten them that way. After that we all went to the Krech's for rice and chili, and played charades afterward. The fellows really enjoyed it. Murphy was the most pleasant drunk imaginable. They are a great bunch of guys. I hate to see them go. And the Krechs are great, too. Glad they are still here.

Putting on a play requires a good working relationship among the whole group, like a sports team – closeness, awareness of the others' roles (literally), a lot of give and take. In fact, as director I encouraged the actors to forget their military status and become their character even in "Mister Roberts" where they might be themselves but in a special way. It was necessary to get to know them to some depth, what their inhibitions were, how far they could "stretch" to become a character, and how much they could develop on their own.

One of the fellows from VS-25 Squadron, Floyd Castillo, tall and blond, had a good voice and nice appearance, but had no idea how to play a part. However, he could imitate. He was cast as one of the sailors in "Mister Roberts." I acted the role, he watched and listened, and then he could "play it back." And it worked fine in the performance.

It was Castillo who first called me by my first name, sort of a slip of the tongue. Inadvertently it was Sarge who enabled it. His name, Sargent, made everyone think he was a sergeant, maybe a Marine, or on assignment from the army. At rehearsals and any other time we could, Sarge and I wore civilian clothes; there were no insignias or identification. Naturally I called him by his first name and at rehearsals the enlisted men picked up on it; he became "Sarge" to them. Sarge called me "Don" as did the other officers and the women. It wasn't long before Castillo let

"Don" slip out, several times in rehearsal. But it was still "Mr. Connolly" for the rest of them.

In San Francisco, the four of us in the apartment had been on a first name basis with a young chief and another enlisted man from the office and with Chief Nielsen from OCS; we had invited them and their wives to our apartment for dinner, and saw them on other social occasions.

Out here, under the continuous military presence, breaking protocol took on a different dimension. It was easier for an officer to use a first name. An officer's concern had to be for the enlisted men, that they might become used to a relationship that could backfire on them if not supported by the officer.

Senior officers usually don't approve of it, at least officially. Even some junior officers feel that way; some are disturbed if they themselves are called by their first name by an officer junior to them. I'm a reserve; maybe that accounts for my attitude. We "civilians in uniform" aren't "military" enough to suit a lot of standards. Within our Coast Guard group, a certain amount of protocol is observed, and discipline is maintained; but it is achieved through reason, not by rules. There's no attempt to put on the military dog.

I felt my first name was as much a title of friendship as "sir" is a title of respect. Perhaps a name is only a sign of familiarity, since "sir" is often said in contempt. One idea kept popping up – "here are guys my own age, guys I'd be bumming around with, calling me 'sir'."

At one of the beach parties I suggested to Santiago that he drop the Mr. Connolly stuff. Very innocently he said, "What'll I call you?" "How about Don?" was my answer. He was delighted as a kid. Just before his squadron departed I went to say good-bye and take him some pictures of the party. Then I was "Mr. Connolly." Possibly out of deference to the presence of other men, or just force of habit.

Castillo hadn't attended any of the beach parties; my "first name" was on his own. One day in the Administration Building I chewed him out for not going to the party. He had no excuse, except that, very honestly, he usually didn't have much fun in a big crowd. Then he apologized for calling me "Don." I told him to forget about it, that at the right times and places it was alright with me. Well, he used "Mr. Connolly" a little longer, then it was "Don" completely. When we started the full production, the others, Crowley, for example, got it from him.

Crowley started in almost immediately, but never once slipped at the proper times. Pretty soon all the enlisted men in the cast were doing it. And I was glad. Pride, perhaps. Conceit. In a reverse kind of way. But they were Floyd and Jim and Walt and Stek to me – and I was Don to them.

27 October 1953
Dear Ma and all —

It's been a long day in the office. We've had an incident -- an appendicitis aboard a merchant ship – that has kept me busy all day. It started at midnight last night when we first got the word, and even now at 8:30 p.m. it's still hanging fire. We flew some supplies to the ship, dropped them by parachute. The action itself is simple, but it takes so long to get the information necessary to get the operation going.

Perhaps I have given the idea that Guam is completely primitive. This is by no means the case. Being a U.S. possession, it is trying to imitate us commercially. The several large communities have stores – clothes, hardware, auto repair, dairy queen, record shops, etc. – as well as movies, taverns and dance halls. There is a daily paper on the island, also. The markets are fairly nice, but all pretty expensive – about twice as high as in the states. There are about a half-dozen traffic lights. The weather is rough on the cars, so most of them are in poor condition. The Jeep is the usual family car. As is to be expected, the chief source of income for the island is the military, in both what is paid to the islanders it hires and in what the military personnel spend.

Also included in the letter is the statement *I finally got in to see the captain*. There's no record of the date that occurred, but it was a watershed event. It, and what ensues, requires a chapter or two of their own.

Chapter Twelve

A Real Little Theatre
A Little Real Theatre
A Little Theatre, Really?

The Little Theatre is going ahead. How, I don't know, and sometimes, I wonder why. I put in the letter to the captain for funds, etc., and heard no reply. Lieutenant Commander Laing, the Exec, was not able to bring about any action on it – not that he tried. He won't ever push anything. Finally I went to see the captain myself.

There's no record or recollection of what lead up to that decision, "to see the captain myself." Was there some Coast Guard input, official or friendly? Did I ask Commander McCaffery for his advice? He had advised me to contact the Navy Executive Officer at the very beginning, and that was important to our success so far. Maybe it just seemed the only way to make something happen. I was Coast Guard, the Navy was in charge; I was an ensign, not usually given much regard by a captain. However it happened, it was a momentous moment in the life of the NAS Little Theatre, Agana, Guam. So momentous that the meeting is vividly etched in my memory.

I made an appointment with the captain's secretary, Chief Matthews, and arrived on time, maybe a little early.

Chief Matthews informed the captain I was waiting. I waited a little longer; then he told Matthews to get Lieutenants Morris and Stegall (the old and new special services officers) to come up. They came up and Lieutenant Commander Maris, the administrative assistant (or flunky) came in, too.
The four of us entered Captain Gazze's office . . .

The office was on the second floor of the administrative building, so located, apparently, for the view of the ocean or for the breeze that would keep the place cool. But there were no windows to be seen. A heavy drape covered the wall behind the large, tidy mahogany desk where Captain Silvius Gazze, USN, was sitting. He was nice-looking, with silver-gray hair and chiseled features that now bore a serious, no-nonsense mien.

The floor was carpeted wall-to-wall, and the walls were paneled in a dark wood. An air-conditioner droned in the corner, in a cut in the wall, necessary not only for the comfort of the captain but to prevent mildew and decay in the décor. Various naval artifacts, photos and certificates filled appropriate spaces.

The letter requesting the $500 to start the theatre was on the desk in front of the captain.

I was able to study and remember all these elements while listening to the captain's dissertation.

. . . and stood in a semi-circle in front of Captain Gazze's desk – two of us with hands held in front, two with hands in back. He started talking about the theatre that "Ensign Connolly has running loose on the station." He then got on to the subject of economy and long-range planning. Seems there's going to be a big theatre here "someday" and he'd rather put money in that. Then we got around to picking up coke bottles and saving money that way. Then came a sea-story about Adak that had some slight reference to the theatre.

Morris just stood there nodding his head and agreeing with everything the captain said. Maybe that's the way to be, but right now he seems like a big horse's ass. He leaves in a few days – maybe things will pick up.

So far no one else had spoken or moved. I found myself checking everyone's expressions and postures, hoping for a sign of encouragement. My hands got tired and dropped to my side.

There were more stories about the difficulties of a project like this – safety, for example. You got to have curtains and they might catch on fire. I explained that for The Scenes we used discarded tow target materials and treated them with a fire-proof solution. And what about participation? People here, well, can they really do something like this? The captain had not attended the production of The Scenes in September, so I told him about the performances and how the audiences had responded.

No one added a comment.

Then he summarized his major objections:

"I like going to the theatre, and I don't mind spending $7.50 for a ticket on Broadway, but how good can anything out here be?"

And, picking up the letter with the request for funds: "I'm not going to approve any blank check for $500. There's no way that's going to happen."

With nothing more to say, he looked from one to the other of us arced in front of him. By this time I was feeling drained and helpless. When no one else spoke, it was obvious it was up to me.

"Captain, all I know is, without your okay, I can't get any help from anyone."

That was all. Somehow I knew to shut my mouth and say no more.

The captain looked from me to all the others, then to the letter of request. He had heard nothing from anyone other than me for or against it. A pause with furrowed brow seemed interminable.

"Well – " There was another pause.

Finally: "Okay – go ahead. But you submit a chit for every item you want; I'll have to approve it – personally." He looked at me and Lieutenant Morris, who was still bobbing his head like it was on a string. "Every item."

I nodded, too. "Yes, sir."

"Go ahead, but keep the spending low."

"Yes, sir. Thank you, sir."

The meeting, the interview, was over and we all started to leave. Lieutenant Morris gave me a little nod and I shrugged a little smile.

"Say," the captain said, and we all stopped. "Who do we play tonight?"

"The Sun Devils."

"Where are they from?"

I recalled that Morris had told me the captain spent $100 each week to put signs on the sides of the station buses to advertise the football games.

That was enough – I left this patron of sports and the arts and went my not-so-merry way.

News of the captain's reluctant and qualified okay was welcomed by the theatre group. We had a nucleus of the actors from The Scenes, and most were anxious to put on the full play. Some had left – my Harriet – and a few said they wouldn't have the time. And we would need to fill other roles, characters that were not in the scene we had done. It was the middle of October and we needed to either find a stage (not likely) or build it somewhere and rehearse and produce and light a three-act play with eighteen speaking roles plus non-speaking criminals and deputies, delivery men, and a young girls' choir.

"The Man Who Came to Dinner" was the most ambitious of the three plays we had done in The Scenes. The play opened on Broadway in 1939 and ran for 739 performances. Some of its characters are based on real people connected with the theatre – literary lion and theatre critic Alexander Woollcott was the model for Sheridan Whiteside, the "Man" of the title; other major roles were based on Noel Coward, Harpo Marx and Gertrude Lawrence. In 1942, it was made into a film with Monty Woolley, the original Whiteside on stage, supported by Bette Davis, Ann Sheridan, Billie Burke, and Jimmy Durante. Those roles required some sophistication, while the people of Mesalia, Ohio and the home of Mr. and Mrs. Ernest Stanley were quite ordinary and naïve by comparison.

The story is this: Whiteside, a famous critic and radio personality, is on a lecture tour and accepts an invitation for lunch at the Stanley home – a great honor for them. It's early December and he slips on a patch of ice on their steps and is diagnosed with a broken hip. He's laid up recuperating, and his usual eccentricities and vanity become intolerable.

He turns the household upside down, demands special food and cigarettes, ties up the house phone with calls from famous people throughout the world offering condolences and words of cheer, and receives outrageous gifts from some of them. Whiteside relies totally on his secretary, Maggie, who has put up with his quirks for many years and seems doomed to end up on the romantic scrap heap, until she meets a Mesalia newspaperman and budding playwright, Bert, who strikes a spark and they get serious. When Whiteside learns she's going to leave him to marry Bert, he calls in an aging but glamorous actress looking for a new play, who, Whiteside hopes, will break up the romance. And he is visited by a British writer-actor who despises the actress, and a clown who will stop at nothing to pull a prank or help a friend.

During all of this, the household is trying to lead normal lives, but Whiteside interferes there as well, encouraging a daughter to elope with a union organizer and a son to follow his dream of a career in photography. And Whiteside insists on entertaining a group of prison inmates (he specializes in weird crimes) and on broadcasting his annual soupy, sappy Christmas Eve radio message from the Stanley living room, complete with sound engineers and a girls' choir. Of course, there is an idiot Stanley sister living upstairs who continually gives Whiteside little gifts. The citizens, including the local physician, try to experience his public charm only to be rebuffed and humiliated.

In addition to the many and diverse roles, the action calls for a crazy range of props from medical equipment – wheelchair, x-rays, trays and bottles – to an ant colony, broadcast equipment and a mummy case big and strong enough to cart the actress away in. In the second act a decorated, lighted Christmas tree appears.

The set is the living room of the Stanley home, with a staircase at the back and many doors. The time is winter so non-Guam clothing would be needed for a number of characters.

My personal strong suit was my familiarity with the play and the confidence that it would go over well "even on Guam." Maybe it would take magic of some kind to make everything fall into place, but that can happen, right?

Right.

But then, there's Guam Fever.

I keep waiting for the seasons to change. But nothing ever happens. Trees are the same color, the same flowers are blooming. It's the same place all the time. The warmth is nice but fatiguing after any exercise. No wonder the people are as slow-moving as they are.

Guam Fever, waiting to happen.

The Plan of the Day announced performance dates of December 8, 9, 10 and 11, the need for actors and a date for tryouts, and a call for production people to build sets and get props. It didn't mention the need for lights and curtains; they would come from "somewhere," just like our stage.

(Continuing from the letter of Oct 27)
I finally got into see the captain about the theatre – would he okay some money for us? He said he'd okay small amounts, but would not give us a flat sum. So we are going ahead and try to build the stage on our own. Another captain who is also on the station, but who is not in the same chain of command as Gazze (our captain) is thoroughly behind us. He has some influence, so we are using that. Quite a few enlisted men have begun showing interest – so building the stage shouldn't be difficult. Please keep up the prayers.

Captain O.P. Smoot was that other captain. His wife gathered props for The Scenes, and both attended and thoroughly enjoyed them. He gave us encouragement at every turn.
But he couldn't provide us with a stage.
Maybe it was the prayers, maybe some angels assigned to theatre projects were at work, or maybe only a couple of phone calls were involved – someone, probably Lieutenant Commander Laing, gave me the lead: "Go see Lieutenant Commander Livingston – he runs the armory."

The armory was the largest interior space on the air station, besides the hangers. The building was a Quonset, 40 feet wide, twice the width and height of our "old" theatre, with seating for several hundred people on wooden benches with sloped backs and curved seats. It was used for classes about firearms, which were stored in a large room at the far end, behind a small platform about 8x8 and two feet high that held a white plywood-sized vertical panel that served as a projection screen.

Lieutenant Commander Livingston was the officer-in-charge, short, red-headed and pugnacious looking, a "mustang" who had come up through the enlisted ranks. I had never met the man, but he was my only contact so he was my first stop in the search for a space to build a stage.

His office was one of the cubicles on either side of the door just inside the armory. He was standing there when I went in, and I introduced myself.

"Commander Livingston," (I had learned to use the higher part of a multiple-word rank) "I'm Ensign Connolly. Commander Laing said I should come and see you – "

He nodded once.

"Un-huh."

I detected a southern accent.

"Uh – to see you, sir, about maybe using the armory to put on plays for –"

"Un-huh. Ah thank it's a fahn idea."

I stopped to process what I thought I had heard. Did he say, "I think it's a fine idea"? Did he know all that would be involved? How could he?

"Sir, I'm talking about building a stage for the Little Theatre – in the armory –"

"Ah thank it's a fahn idea."

This was too easy.

I remember staring at him a few moments. I wanted to be sure he understood that we would totally transform the instructional end of the space. The postage-stamp platform would be replaced by a stage across the entire width of the building, about 4 feet high, with a proscenium wall -- How do I say that?

"Well, Commander, you realize, sir, we'd build a stage – "

"Of course, I do. I never went to college, or nothin' like that, but I know two and two make four."

Amazingly, my first stop was my only stop.

It soon became obvious that that was his mantra: "I never went to college, but – " It preceded most of his replies when he learned, step by step, what we were going to do <u>next</u>! "Learned" – because I took him at face value and didn't ask any more questions. When construction got going, I just checked in with him and told him what seemed appropriate.

Whoever on the Navy side had prepared the way, he must have worked magic because it didn't seem likely that Lieutenant Commander Livingston would easily and quickly surrender his military bastion to the arts. I like to think it was Lieutenant Commander Laing. It totally redeems him from all my thoughts that he could have done more to support us. I had to learn that people would first do what was expected of them, and then more, if they could, but do it in their own way.

Captain Gazze had said, "Go ahead, etc." Lieutenant Stegall, the new Special Services Officer, didn't give the movement much hope and told me so. No doubt he was being honest, realistic; he might have seen projects like this die before blooming. Maybe it was the kind of activity he was sorry it was his to inherit. In any case, he never gave any support.

But old optimistic me went ahead; my optimism was more than justified.

Joe Gulde, a Navy hut mate from Notre Dame whose family was in the construction business in Amarillo, was an Ensign in Public Works. He had architectural skills and had volunteered to draw up plans for a stage if we ever built one.

I went to Joe and asked him about the plans, when could he have them finished? That was on a Thursday; he said, probably next Wednesday. A whole week, and it was only about six or seven weeks until production.

Before tryouts for the full production, I called the people who had come to The Scenes and filled out a form for comments, interest and such. One of those was a Parachute Rigger 3rd Class named Jim Crowley – short (oops, my size), dark hair, a true Mick with a lot of talk and appreciation for the occasional Pint. He came to The Scenes by accident and filled out a form. He tried out for "The Man" and got the part of Banjo, a cigar-smoking combination of the Marx Brothers who provides much of the antics in the play.

Crowley was a friend of Walt Hagen BU2, a SeaBee turned

Shore Patrolman and rifle instructor, a friend, most likely, because Hagen in his off-time was a bartender at the enlisted club and Crowley was a frequent patron. "SeaBee" is a cute phonetic version of the initials of the Construction Battalion, the branch of the Navy that builds things.

Hagen by some chance was on the Master-at-Arms force on the station. The first time I met him was at an M-1 rifle indoctrination class. Sarge and I had been told to attend, so we did. Hagen was responsible for indoctrinating the men new to the station in marching, carrying the rifle and accompanying skills.

That meant he wasn't doing anything related to construction.

At the moment.

Chapter Thirteen

The Rescue Business

2 November 1953

The rescue business took a quick upswing a few weeks ago. Had five incidents in three days. The admiral of the 14th Coast Guard District was here on an acquaintance trip at the time and some expressed the thought that we had staged it all to impress him. A Jap weather man was evacuated by plane in bad weather from Marcus Island, we had three intercepts (planes with bad engines request escort, we go meet them and follow them in – that's an intercept) and one near drowning. The fellow we saved from drowning lives with Sarge and me – sort of gave the rescue a personal touch.

The fellow was Ray Davis.

About two weeks ago Ray, a friend of his from another naval station, and I went swimming on a Sunday afternoon. Sarge had the duty at the rescue center. We had just been visited by Typhoon "Alice" which brought much rain and wind. The sea was still pretty rough – the waves were higher than I'd ever seen them. Ray and Bill and I went a little way into the surf and were bouncing around in the waves. Because of the reef, the sea swells usually don't come all the way to the shore and this change was particularly inviting. Ray was of a mind to try to get through the breakers as we had done before when things were much, much calmer. After about five minutes we realized the current was too strong to get through; so after playing around a little while longer, Bill and I headed for shore.
The current resulting from the waves was almost overpowering even as close in as we were, and it took us a little while to make the shore. When Bill and I got safely on the beach, I looked around for Ray and saw him out among the waves. He had been talking about trying to get through them, so I figured he had made it. Bill and I sat and talked for a while, and I saw Ray wave. I waved back. Then I heard him yell. Right away I was sure something was wrong – but I didn't hear any-

thing more, so I forgot about it. Especially when I saw him wave again.

We got up and started walking down the beach, and who should be there but the Krechs. Shep said somebody was in trouble in the surf and somebody on the beach was going for help. I said, "No, that's Ray out there. He's all right." But they were sure he was in trouble and it was obvious he wasn't getting any closer to shore. Some men were going for help anyway, so I went with them.

The men got some lifeguards at a near-by beach; from there I called the rescue center. Sarge got a plane off as soon as possible and got the Marine Land Rescue Team into action. They are volunteers who have a truck and use a motor-powered life raft to rescue swimmers. It took 15 or 20 minutes for the plane to get there. All that time I was just standing there watching from a distance, feeling helpless and guilty. If Ray was in trouble (and I wasn't sure yet that he was) this was the best course of action. But if he wasn't, and all this equipment was expended, and if word got around that he was outside the reef just for "fun," there could be serious repercussions.

The plane finally arrived. I called Sarge on the phone – I just couldn't stand by and not know what was going on. He had the plane on radio. It worked out that I would tell Sarge if the plane was looking in the right place. He would relay the info to the plane. The plane sighted some paddle boards, but couldn't see anybody in the water. I told Sarge that the lifeguards had brought paddleboards with them, and that the plane was in the right place.

Then the plane spotted him. They made a couple of passes and then dropped a raft. It was a good drop – landed about 8 yards away. Ray climbed in. Then a lifeguard who had managed to get through the breakers on a paddleboard got to him. The Marines got through the surf, got them in tow and brought them ashore.

There was a big crowd around by that time, taking pictures, making comments. Ray held his fins in front of his face as he walked ashore. He was put in an ambulance and taken to the hospital. He was scratched from the coral on his arms and legs and his stomach. Also full of water. Also very lucky. He's one of the few to come out breathing.

Ray's story was this: He lost sight of Bill and me; then he saw Bill, but thought that I might have been caught in the undertow. While looking around for me, he was struck by a wave and the next thing he knew he was being dragged over the coral out to sea. He ended up in the middle of the breakers; to keep from being dashed to pieces on the coral, he had to swim even farther out. He got loaded with salt water and was vomiting all the time. The waves had knocked his face mask off, but he still had his swim fins, which kept him up. All the time he said he was calm, because he knew I'd know who to get for help. He was only worried how long it would take me to realize he was in trouble. His swimming suit was partially ripped.

He was well aware that a deliberate attempt to get beyond the reef could mean a court martial. But his story laid everything to accident, so he was safe. It is possible that he thought he could get through the waves and deliberately swam out there. But I guess I'll never know. There have been no repercussions.

His captain had him write up his story and had it printed in the station paper, for the benefit of others. He wrote checks for all who had a part in his rescue. His exterior has not changed, except he dare not kid us about the Coast Guard. I was afraid I was going to have to write a letter beginning, "Dear Mrs. Davis, I last saw your son – "

One big reason, other than ordinary humanity, that I was so concerned over his rescue was that he has given up his Catholic faith due to rigid self-indoctrination as well as the influence of Harvard. The boy who got to him on the paddleboard made the sign of the cross before he got in the water. I told him I had been praying for him while he was out there. He answered: "I thought about all that while I was out there. I guess if my principles weren't as strong as they are, I would have prayed, too." He's still breathing, so he's got another chance coming.

That rescue gave me a healthier attitude toward my job. It's very easy to get lax and complacent just sitting in the center day after day. When the phone rings you get the attitude that it's interrupting your reading or letter-writing. I now have a more personal attachment and affection for this place. It makes the hours spent here a little more bearable.

 . . . This has just about developed into a book. It is now November 4. No I haven't been writing all this time. I had to quit on the 2nd. And yesterday the CG had a picnic which took up the day and rehearsal took up the night. The picnic was great – broiled steaks and swimming. I was with a Coastie Lieutenant who is in the play, a nice guy named Omar Cowles (pronounced without the "w"). I went home with him *and had dinner with his wife and two kids. You know, this is Be Kind to Bachelor Officers' week.*

I am now red from the sun, and tired from the duty, but most finally, I am Connolly on Guam. Oh well, time will soothe the heat and the weariness, and I guess, the Guam. A happy Thanksgiving to you all. Observe one minute's silence on Nov. 25. I will have been in the service one year.

Gad!

Love to all – Don

Chapter Fourteen

The Play: Making It Happen

With the word that we had a Little Theatre, at least on paper, or more accurately, from the mouth of Captain Gazze, our group had to shift gears and rev our engines to get back into a rehearsal schedule. Guam Fever had not taken center stage but it was lurking in the wings, so it took a strong dose of optimism and determination to get everybody going again, and to find actors for the replacements and additional roles.

Along with the announcement of the dates for the performances, additional try-outs were scheduled. When someone came who really wasn't suitable, it was difficult to say "no" because maybe no one better would come along. Cast members brought others they thought would be good, some who wanted to be there and some who didn't. A big concern for me about every prospect was their willingness and ability to commit to a pretty concentrated schedule; we would perform in about six weeks and we didn't need any dropouts as we had had with The Scenes.

That proved too much to ask.

It was a plus that we had done the scene from the play, that most of those actors were still with us, and they had their characters pretty well set. Lloyd George had been an outstanding Whiteside with the right mixture of vanity and charm, sarcasm and wit. As the leading lady, Ann Shay, playing Whiteside's secretary, Maggie Cutler, drew on her family situation as the mother of three young children and had the right combination of detachment and control. Jan Yost would repeat her role as the actress, Lorraine Sheldon, and Dick Hollands his role as her nemesis, the British writer-actor, Beverly Carlton.

As Mr. and Mrs. Stanley who hosted Whiteside, Phyllis Laing and Commander John Barron showed the general feelings of anxiety and frustration, but would need work, as would Grover Thomas, an enlisted man, and Donna McCarthy, a civilian worker, as the Stanleys' son and daughter. And dependable, faithful Sarge would repeat the bumbling Dr. Bradley, and Teresa Crider the harassed but indomitable nurse, Miss Preen.

We had lost the idiot sister, Harriet Stanley and John, the butler. Finding a replacement for her especially would not be easy.

For the "new" characters, Omar Cowles, my CG pilot colleague, said he'd do the newspaperman, Bert Jefferson, and enlisted man Jim Crowley was firm as Banjo. Jim's parachute-rigger partner, Rinald Steketee, was talked into playing the butler. Two officers' wives, Maggie McDuffie and Ann Scanland, signed on to play the neighbors who bring gifts to Whiteside – important first-scene roles that start the comic action.

There was one other role – the German scientist, Professor Metz, who brings Whiteside an ant colony as a gift; it was a small character part and required an accent, so it fell to me.

Ray Davis decided his work in "Mister Roberts" had satisfied any theatrical urges and decided not to get involved.

Rehearsals were held in the "old" theatre where we had done The Scenes – a much smaller space than we would need for the full production, but big enough to do some blocking, learn the lines and develop the characters – until we got on the "big" stage.

There were many threads to be laced together.

From the November 2 letter:

The play is coming along fairly well. We have yet to build our stage; but the blueprints should be finished today, and there is a SeaBee who is going to do most of it. The production dates are Dec 8, 9, 10, 11. It's going to be a tight schedule, but that makes the time pass all the quicker. The actors are just about at the point where they know their lines. Hope they learn them all quickly.

I'm making sure I know the part of Whiteside again. The Australian who is playing Whiteside has shown certain traits that could prove disastrous. He's a nice guy and has sufficient character to see a thing like this through. However, he doesn't like this play for us to be doing. Thinks it's too sophisticated. His job here is not a hard one –

only works a couple of days out of the week. He has gotten in the habit of taking things so easy that he finds it rather hard to confine himself to the schedule I set up. He complained about the same things during rehearsals for the scenes we did. However, he fits the part so perfectly and is very amusing in his own way, and quite frankly I couldn't do without him. I'm trying to prepare for any emergency.

I first became aware of my Australian, Lloyd, at my first "Fight Night" at the O'Club. Mosiman took me; we sat at the bar and he pointed out various people and told me what they did. A tall, bushy-haired mustached man was dancing and smiling with an attractive woman.

"That's Lloyd George. He's Australian – works for QANTAS. Takes care of the Australian troops."

His name made me cock my head and smile – same as the famous British prime minister; "Any relation?" I wanted to ask, but said, "Is that his wife?"

"No, he's not married. He dances with the officers' wives."

Then he showed up to audition for The Scenes, played two parts very well, and it was clear that his talent would carry "The Man Who" a long way. We had worked together building the set pieces for that first production and had become friends. He was ten or twelve years older than I, so at 33 or 35 certainly not old (although he looked older) and loved the arts of any kind. He had to adjust his thinking about Americans when he realized that some of us knew quite a bit about the literature and arts he presumed were meaningful only to members of the Empire.

In keeping with my youthful, American familiarity and the slang of the time, I occasionally called him "Dad." Nothing paternal, just another version of "hey, man" or "oh boy." He put up with it for a while, then firmly instructed me, "I'm not your father."

He shared a small Quonset with his mechanic. On a wall in their living area was a picture of the new queen, Elizabeth II. When he answered the phone, his greeting was, "Qantas Empire Airways, George speaking."

The rehearsal schedule for the full production began with Act One, going through it for basic blocking and then breaking it into "sections" according to the participants, so that people weren't hanging around with little to do. Then that was repeated for Act Two and Act Three. The problem for Lloyd was that he was on stage most of the play and was needed for most rehearsals.

That requirement plus his sense that a lot of the other actors (maybe all of them) couldn't pull off the needed sophistication affected his enthusiasm and he began to miss rehearsals. Someone else would sit in his wheelchair and read his lines.

My Australian friend didn't show up one night for rehearsal ("slightly under") and I was fuming. That was a Thursday night. The next night we didn't have rehearsal. That afternoon I called him and said I'd like to talk to him sometime before rehearsal Saturday afternoon. He said Saturday noon would be best.

I saw him Friday night at the Officers' Club and politely ignored him. By Saturday noon I had simmered down a bit and told him politely he was fouling up the works. It wasn't fair to the rest of the cast, nor to himself, to miss rehearsals. As it is, he has to miss some due to planes arriving from Australia or Japan, and that is bad enough.

When he told me that he didn't think the play was right for our actors or our audience, I assured him it would work, that it had played well with high school actors for the unsophisticated Midwest folk of St. Louis, Missouri. I repeated my confidence that he could do the role beautifully and that I knew he didn't need all the rehearsals but that the other actors did, and he had to be there for them because only by hearing his delivery of the lines and seeing his expressions would they be able to react properly – and after all, re-acting is what acting is all about.

On top of that, I reminded him that I had played the role only five years before, could easily re-learn the lines and if necessary, I would, and I would play the part. It was up to him.

That was just the first of the dips in *"the play coming along fairly well."*

Jan Yost was too young to play Lorraine Sheldon, an actress who has seen better days, on the prowl for a good play and the playwright as well.

Jan is still seeing her good days so we made her a sexy, conceited actress. She had played the part before, and on top of that, she has a natural, casual sexy quality. However, if you made some comment about it, she would seem offended. In rehearsal she liked to be told that she was doing well, but if you told her that, she'd louse up the next time. So I'd tell her one part was good, but that something else wasn't; that got what we both wanted.

There was no doubt she would do the part well and be a strong presence on stage. In addition to her looks she had a good sense of timing and delivery, all laced with enough temperament to give me a few headaches. In the play, Whiteside gets rid of Lorraine by having her carried out in a mummy case and shipped to Nova Scotia. Jan at first didn't want to get into the case (even though it was upright); it's a climactic moment in the play, very funny, and gives a lift to the final minutes. She eventually changed her mind, played the moment very dramatically, and let the case shut and be carried off with her inside. It was a great exit.

A more serious situation developed after her husband Paul returned from a trip to Tokyo as the aide to the Coast Guard admiral on his inspection visit. Paul had caught a bad cold and at rehearsal I made some (what I thought) innocuous comment about catching a cold in a fun place like Tokyo. Jan didn't show up for the next rehearsal nor the one after that, and probably several more. I was totally in the dark about any problem and too busy with the stage and other things to think it was anything more than catching up after his time away.

When I was on duty in the Rescue Center, Paul came in and said he wanted to meet me in my hut after my duty, had something he wanted to talk to me about. Fortunately I was alone when he came. He explained that Jan had been upset by my "joke" that he might have played around in Tokyo.

"She takes that kind of thing very seriously," I remember him saying. "I know you didn't mean anything by it. And I know she wants to be in the play. I'll talk to her and I'm sure she'll come back. I just wanted to warn you not to say anything about it."

It was an amazing adult, gentlemanly encounter, just matter-of-fact and open: Paul had weighed the situation, knew what the outcome should be, and did what was appropriate. It was a strong lesson for me – once again my lighthearted banter had been troubling to someone else, and it almost cost me the production. A replacement for her would have been impossible to find.

No wonder Admiral Paul A. Yost, Jr. became Commandant of the Coast Guard in 1986.

Omar Cowles, the CG pilot, had been friendly with Sarge and me from the start. He was a tall, young- and good-looking guy with a crew cut, very slim but well-proportioned. His family was over with him – a vivacious wife and two good kids. Several people had made reference to his wild ways before his wife arrived on the island, and through the acquaintance we built up I found it was true. He more or less told me himself. But I've learned to take people for what they are now and hope that the present and the future may be a little better.

I called Omar on a hunch one day when I was getting desperate for somebody to play Bert Jefferson, the romantic interest. Omar fit the part perfectly in looks and personality, and I told him so. I also said that it was a personality part, and not much acting ability was needed. He said he'd give it a try, and for a while he did wonderfully in it.

We had been in rehearsal a couple of weeks when he said he was going to Hong Kong for a week to do Christmas shopping. He missed a couple of rehearsals before leaving, and when the time came for him to return, I heard nothing from him. So I called his wife and she said he was returning the next day. She asked how he was doing and I assured her that everything would turn out okay. She said she thought she would come to rehearsals so she could help him out, and they could be together. She was teaching school and wasn't home with him during the day.

Another couple of days passed and still no word from Omar. I was talking to the Air Detachment one day at work and asked if Omar had returned. He had and they called him to the phone. After a few pleasantries about the trip, he said he didn't know if he would be able to do the part – the watch schedule had been changed to his disadvantage and that had greatly upset him. I told him the predicament he would put me in if he quit, with opening about two weeks away. So he said he'd think about it and let me know before next rehearsal. Two days later I hadn't heard anymore, so I called him again. He was still undecided. Finally I told him I'd have to know one way or the other, hoping he would come my way.

He said he'd better forget about it all together.

Ann Shay, playing the secretary, Maggie Cutler, had been with us since The Scenes in August and was always on the lookout for actors. She recruited Jewel Williams to play Harriet Stanley, the idiot sister.

Jewel is medium size with a very small voice and very pretty face, too pretty and well-developed for the part. I'd try to get her to "float" when she walks. I'd show her how and say "float, float" when she tried it. She was too stiff, it seemed, and had no concept of using her voice to make it wistful.

Not only was she too pretty, even worse, she couldn't let herself get into the character. Every movement seemed awkward, as if she was locked into an unbreakable mold.

Still, she was all we had.

Teresa Crider, (Tess), playing Miss Preen, was a native Hawaiian and had the "aloha" pleasantness of the islands. She had been very good in The Scenes and it was a big plus to have her in the full production. She was short and overweight, a good visual contrast to the rest of the cast.

She had money, she told me, as had her husband; her family was in Honolulu where she was born, and she and hubby were in continuous strife because she didn't want to go back there yet and he did. He was with a civilian agency and they lived on the air station. They had three kids – hers, too, I guess, but she is only 22.

One day when I called her to tell her about rehearsals, she was out and I talked to her husband instead. About a half-hour later he called back and asked me if I could get Tess to quit the play. He felt she had become preoccupied with the play, and she wasn't taking care of the kids properly, hadn't bathed them at night, left them before the baby sitter arrived. I didn't want to lose her in the part but didn't want to aggravate family relationships.

Before I could deal with it, nature took its course: one of the kids got measles and she had to quit. So we were without a Miss Preen.

Ann Shay herself was a pretty calm and steadying force, most of the time, reassuring me, when needed, that things would work out. She was tall with dark red hair pulled back and hanging to her shoulders, a fairly angular face that showed strength and sensitivity. She never missed a rehearsal and was willing to help in any way she could.

The trouble came when her husband, Dick, who had been sent to Japan, didn't get back to Guam when she thought he was going to. Commander Barron, "Mr. Stanley" of the play, was the skipper of her husband's squadron, with the power to send or bring back any man in VU-5. Barron was not the most understanding man in the world and in trying to be funny would often anger Ann. Ann was a typical Navy wife, most anxious to further her husband's career, but at the same time wanted him around all the time. Usually she spoke her mind, which could have been to her husband's detriment.

All this, you understand, had no direct effect on me except that when she was emotionally disturbed, rehearsal did not go very well; or I would have to ask Barron when he was leaving for Japan (pretending I wanted to know what rehearsals he'd be missing) so she could judge when Dick would return. She always had some worry about the kids or that Barron had listened in on her radio talk with Dick in Japan.

One evening after rehearsal, a few weeks before opening, Ann said she needed to talk to me. With all the variables swirling at the moment – building the stage, filling the cast, not messing up relations with the Navy – I felt nothing could surprise me.

Was I wrong.

"Don, I think you should know, I'm pregnant. Probably a couple of months."

So here was this lady, playing a middle-aging, emotionally-hardened, non-romantic secretary, about ready to "pop."

There was no option to get another actress, nor did either one of us want to. I had come to rely on the solid foundation she brought and the respect she had from all the others as well.

She looked at me and shrugged. We would just have to hope for the best. Not showing – yet – but it was anybody's guess when that would happen. That would certainly give another dimension to her character.

It was providential that Jim Crowley came into my world on Guam. Not only was he putting his acting talent to work as Banjo, and had been the catalyst for getting Hagen to build the stage, he gathered a lot of other enlisted men into the theatre fold and they gave more of themselves than I had any right to expect.

Enlisted men are a proud bunch. They take pride in their work – in being good whatever-they-are. Sometimes maybe they're too proud – in their attitude toward the "officer." If they feel in any way that they are being discriminated against, they rebel, usually very passively, but nevertheless, they rebel. The attendance at The Scenes bore that out. We announced that the first performance would be by invitation only. That, to them, was discrimination. Only those whose friends were in the scenes showed up either night, or like Crowley, some by accident. It's necessary to win their confidence; to make them know that you are for them. And that's easy to do. Be for them. They don't expect you to lower yourself in your own eyes or in the eyes of your fellow officers. They wouldn't respect you for it.

But they appreciate human consideration; they like to be thought of and about. Somehow, I feel that of the friends I've made in the service, especially on Guam, my better ones are enlisted. Maybe subconsciously I could feel more at ease because I had the gold that told them I was supposed to be somebody; maybe that was it. But no, I don't think so. They've got eyes – and they see all types and can discern pretty easily and quickly. No – I think I like them because they liked me, and I think they liked me because I respected them for what they were, not what they wore. It's not necessary to be coy or funny or self-degrading with them. If you want them to do something for you, ask them. If they do it for you, thank them. And if they ask you something, do it. We're all people, and God help me never to forget it. I will never forget them.

I wrote the above a few weeks after leaving Guam because still firmly embedded in my mind and heart was the dedication and spirit of the guys who contributed so much to the show – the stage we performed on and the performances they gave.

All the preceding has been a kind of prologue to the story of the building of the stage in the NAS Armory. It was done primarily by the enlisted men – Hagen, the brains and most of the labor, with Crowley, Steketee, Castillo, plus Sarge, Lloyd George and myself assisting. They gave their all when needed; they in turn got others to help, if only in supplying us with needed materials. They did a fine job and I'm justly proud of "our" job.

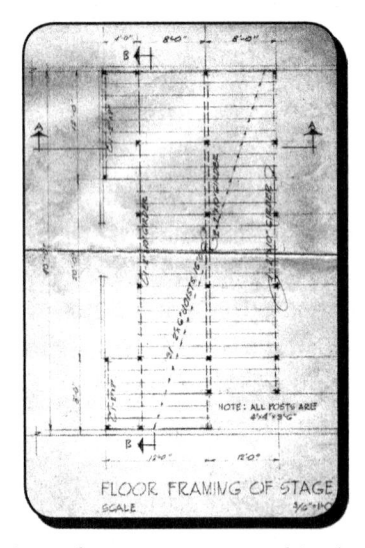

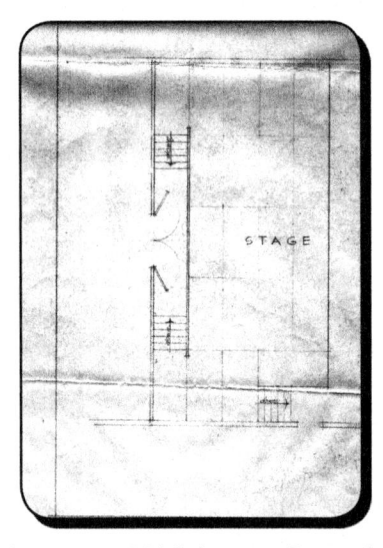

Blueprints of stage constructed in the Armory at NAS Agana, Guam, by BM2 Walt Hagen and the Little Theatre Workers. Blueprints by ENS Joe Gulde, USN

We collected a lot of lumber from the Public Works scrap pile – not scrap but good substantial lumber. Hagen is quite a guy in his own way – his thinly blonded head knows a lot about carpentry. He was figuring out the construction in his own head and figured we had enough. When we got the blueprints from Joe Gulde, we found it wasn't enough; we also found that there was no more of that kind of lumber on the pile. We went ahead building, as we had enough to get started. The stage would be 40 feet wide and 20 feet deep (16 feet in the center to allow for steps to the exit door.)

I found out from the head man at the carpentry shop how much the needed lumber would cost and put in a chit to Captain Gazze for that amount plus the cost of some paint for the scenery and make-up and a few other incidentals. It came to $51.98. We got it – I think the $1.98 did the trick. When I told Gulde about getting the money, he said he had been talking to his boss, Lieutenant Commander McDuffie, about the project and McDuffie said he'd get us what we needed. So we got the lumber free of charge.

Next came plywood. We needed twenty sections. Some of the men living in the Quonsets were being moved to the barracks, so McDuffie said we could tear up the floor in one of the Quonsets and get what we needed. Only they didn't move. So we couldn't tear. Again McDuffie and company came to the rescue and "gave" us the needed lumber. With that the stage flooring was complete.

I made a set of stairs all by myself one afternoon; then all the stairs were in. We started rehearsing on the big stage.

Lieutenant Commander Livingston seemed to be getting cold feet.

He had told me without any persuading that we could use the armory; but in the end he seemed afraid we would go ahead with the project. He gets a kick out of seeing college officers go wrong – "know what I mean?" He would come in and observe the building progress, shake his head and mutter something and leave.

23 November 1953
Dear Mom and all –

I've been meaning to write this for some time. Don't know what held me up. The Little Theatre has been keeping me hopping – we open in two weeks, Dec. 8, and there is still plenty to do. The main part of the stage is now finished. We still have to build the front that separates the stage from the audience – in theatrical jargon, the proscenium. James, you should see what a carpenter I've become. The stage itself is four feet high, 40x20. Really a solid construction. The SeaBee who is building it has taught me a lot; I've tried to be around to help him whenever I can. As you well know, it's no fun doing something like that all by yourself. We have yet to get a Christmas tree – will have to chop something down from around here, I guess. Please say some prayers we have no catastrophes.

Maybe you've read that the CG weather station ships are being taken out of the Atlantic. They are also taking a couple out of the Pacific, and what is more, they are probably going to close up the Search and Rescue stations out here, so far as the CG is concerned – the Navy and Air Force will take them over. There is no official word that we are closing up, but is above the rumor stage. Commander McCaffery should be back from Honolulu today or tomorrow with the final word. There is a chance, however, that just the CG pilots and planes would leave and the controllers (that's me) would stay here. As Jim can explain, there are an infinite number of rumors that can be and usually are concocted when something big is in the wind. Definitely something is going to happen, when and how we don't know. Will be sure to keep you posted.

One afternoon Crowley and I tore up the deck in a Quonset that was finally vacated and we had enough plywood to cover the front of the proscenium arch. That left us with a stage 4 feet high, sixteen feet deep, with wings (the off-stage working area) about 8x20 on each side, and an opening in the front twenty feet wide and ten feet high. And it was all ours. Then it got painted – Public Works did that, also. Then lighting was installed – Commander Barron and VU-5 took care of that. The curtain was made by Crowley and Steketee, both parachute riggers; so were the teasers.

The making of the curtain and the teasers deserves a special mention. Teasers are the covers for the rows of lights that hang above the stage; usually they are black and help keep the audience from noticing where the lighting is coming from. The curtains are what cover the opening of the proscenium before the play and between acts. Nowadays most theatres don't use curtains; the stage is exposed to the audience when they come in.

Regardless of the setup, the usual phrase for starting the play is "the curtain's going up." In truth, if there is a curtain, it usually doesn't go up; it parts – it separates in the middle and is pulled to the sides.

Not in our theatre. We would have a curtain, but we didn't have the track system to pull it apart. Our curtain would use small pulleys and manually "go up."

Rinald Skeketee was Crowley's co-rigger, conscripted by Crowley to join the theatre. Like Crowley, he was also conscripted to play a role, John the butler. The two of them had access to tow targets made of vinyl or polyester, tough materials that were shaped into a long narrow cylinder open at the end behind the towing plane, so it stretched well behind the plane and could be shot at without endangering anybody. Apparently they eventually became obsolete, or surplus. Whatever, they became the material of our teasers and curtain.

A parachute rigger has the equipment to repair the target or make it into something never considered when it was procured. The latter would describe our curtain.

The material was rich red, a bit speckled, but when extended, the redness overwhelmed any variations. Jim and Stek assembled enough to cover our 20x10 proscenium opening, and across the bottom every four or five feet they attached cords that ran vertically to small pulleys (maybe just large "eyes") at the top of the proscenium. All the cords ran to the side where the stage manager could actually "raise the curtain" by the strength of his arms.

I can still recall my excitement, standing in the theatre, when the lights first came on behind the curtain. That massive drape of red just glowed, and so did I. It was Dorothy's ruby slippers. It was the sunset painted on the bottom of the clouds. Somehow I knew it would say to the audience when the lights came on to start the play, this is gonna be something special.

Chapter Fifteen

Besides the Play

My "other life" those final weeks did exist but it became defined by my duty schedule and rehearsal schedule. There was no doubt that I needed another life when so many questions hung in the air about having a finished stage and a full cast by December 8th. Even more important – would Sarge and I still be on Guam on December 8th? There were a lot of loose ends to be tied up. Some roles in the play were in a state of flux. And the two of us played parts in it. It was possible the whole thing would get to the final stages and fall apart.

Even the watch schedule became a respite from the worries of the theatre. Our rescue mission had become almost inconsequential. Since the signing of the armistice in July and the cessation of fighting, ship and plane movements had been reduced. After the burst of activity in mid-November, we had few incidents, occasionally an aircraft intercept or a local vessel in trouble, but nothing major or life threatening. I spent many duty hours writing letters.

It was our responsibility to intercept military aircraft in trouble, and the Navy let us do that when their planes asked for help. Not so the Air Force. Anderson Air Force Base occupied the north end of the island and their planes kept a busy schedule, if only for training. If an Air Force plane heading for Anderson feathered an engine, the Air Force and the Coast Guard would both send out a plane to accompany it home. The thought occurred to me that two rescue planes might collide and in turn would need help.

Sarge's car had arrived and made getting around a lot easier. It was a pre-war Ford, the kind with a rounded back, one of last models made before the auto industry switched to making tanks, trucks and jeeps. It was painted a dull black, a finish I equated with waterproofing material. Sarge was generous in letting me use the car for theatre business – gathering props or incidental building materials or programs from the printer; frequently he was with me and almost indispensable in those endeavors.

Sarge was doing some dating. As noted, he had the gift for meeting people he knew, or who knew people he knew, and dates materialized from that. Some of the dating events were picnics at Tumon or Tarague Beach with the Krechs. Ray Davis was often there too, with his date, Lorraine.

An evening or a picnic with The Krechs continued to be a 'great escape' from the accumulating stresses. They had not yet been moved to navy housing so our visits needed wheels, and I was at the mercy of Sarge or Ray. Frequently all three of us would go together, either to their home or with them to the Naval Hospital Club which provided Nora a break from cooking.

An evening at their home was usually a simple meal preceded by scotch or wine, sometimes followed by bridge, and laced with conversation throughout. They loved to read and usually had a book in progress; conversation frequently was a discussion of a recent one. My reading wasn't on a par with theirs – many of mine had a Catholic theme or subject – so I usually held back and let Ray or Sarge carry it.

One time the subject was comparing Herman Wouk's best seller *The Caine Mutiny* to another naval book, *The Cruel Sea* by Nicolas Monsarrat, both published in 1951. I had read "Caine" and thoroughly enjoyed it, depicting as it did situations that I had experienced in my short time in the military. Ray had read them both and pronounced *The Cruel Sea* to be the better book, more interesting with its British Navy subject and literary flourishes. Nora agreed. Eventually I read it and felt you couldn't compare them because of their differences in scope and size and moral issues.

It was obvious Nora was putting a good face on their life on this remote island. She would rather have been somewhere else; better housing would have helped and that didn't seem to be forthcoming. One evening she was full of excitement over the plans for their new home which had recently arrived by mail. She unrolled the drawings and pointed out the features of this center-hall colonial. It wasn't a grand house; it conformed to the usual design elements of the style but was roomy with extra touches for their lifestyle. And it would fit perfectly on the large property they had purchased on the Wye River near Easton, Maryland.

Wouldn't they miss the excitement of New York? No, their area would provide plenty of socializing with congressmen and D.C. lawyers as neighbors; there would always be books to read, and opportunities for travel in the states and Europe. And New York was just a short trip away.

Nora and I had many conversations, just the two of us. Her family was originally from St. Louis and she was interested in my family and my growing up there. I recognized her family name from real estate signs but it was clear there would have been no connection.

With two of my bothers being chiropractors, she asked about that; I confidently explained the anatomical and neurological principles I had learned from them, with additional commentary about the medical profession's efforts to minimize or destroy their credibility. Somehow I didn't remember at that point that Shep was a member of that profession. Nora never called my attention to it.

With my other brother a priest and my 16 years of Catholic schools, she wanted to talk about religion. Nora and Shep identified themselves as Episcopalians, whether active believers or participants was never revealed. She never expressed her point of view; she just listened patiently to mine.

Early on, to my surprise, she asked if I was still a practicing Catholic.

Why wouldn't I be?

Being Catholic was always and still is part of my life. My family were every-Sunday church-goers who participated in some parish activities. My parents sent all four children to Catholic grade schools and high schools. Our parish was friendly and caring, and like all students we learned the guide book, the Baltimore Catechism, by heart. Those days and until the Second Vatican Council that started in 1961, there were three major sins: eating meat on Friday, missing Mass on Sunday, and doing anything connected with sex (on any day of the week) unless it was within marriage and could lead to procreation.

My Jesuit education in both high school and university had armed me with a lot of information and philosophical principles that could explain and justify just about any areas of concern. It all seemed logical, believable, to me; I was happy to explain it to others, if they were interested.

As I eventually learned, over the years, although I had all sorts of answers, I hadn't even heard a lot of the questions that "lived experience" and maturity will bring you to ask.

My conversations with Nora didn't have the benefit of the large leaps and fine tuning that came from Vatican II and its acknowledgment of personal individuality, its opening up of the Church to the world and other religions, its emphasis on the commonality we share, not the differences that keep us apart. That was eight to twelve years away.

But I was able to show her a letter from the Legion of Decency about the "condemned" rating for the movie "The Moon Is Blue." I had written to them that I had seen the film and found nothing in it that deserved that rating and asked the reason behind it. The reply said that the producer, Otto Preminger, had refused to submit the film for review so they automatically gave it that rating. Basically it said, "He broke the rules <u>so you can see why</u> we had to give the film that rating." Those underlined words I remember.

We both shook our heads over that.

The correspondence course in German had progressed fairly well. It became a good time-filler on watches when there was no activity and I was tired of writing letters. The language was a new challenge, not connected to the Latin and Greek I had studied in school. But I liked words and enjoyed exploring how a language is put together.

Initial enthusiasm resulted in a number of completed lessons in the first weeks, but as the theatre activities developed, my submissions became erratic. There were twenty-five lessons in the program; each one was mailed to USAFI headquarters in Madison, Wisconsin, where they were corrected and mailed back. My "teacher" in Madison was encouraging, so when word came that the Rescue Center might be closed down, I decided to ramp up my efforts and complete the course before we left.

By the end of November there was one lesson to go.

Jim Crowley was a continuous source of support and respite for me. He was confident in his role of Banjo, a natural, handling any comic antics deftly, speaking his lines and twisting his features for comic effect. Whenever he could he helped build the stage, and most important, he and his colleague Skeketee made the front curtain and teasers that completed the look of the stage.

His Irish heritage permeated his being – speech, facial expressions, body language, movement, and the ability to find enjoyment in most situations. He took pleasure in drinking and socializing, and frequently went to the Enlisted Club after rehearsal. One evening he asked if I would like to go with him. I wondered if that would be okay, on both sides of our official "divide," and he said, sure, I would be his guest. I was too tired that night, so we agreed on the next night when we didn't have rehearsal. I would meet him there.

"Civvies best, I guess," I said.

"Sure."

The next evening Jim was sitting at the long bar when I arrived. The club was spacious, and even with groups drinking and laughing at several tables and hanging around the juke box with beers in their hands, it seemed sort of empty. A few of the revelers glanced my way when I came in. I was wearing a Hawaiian-print shirt hanging over civilian trousers. I smiled, a little nervously, went directly to the bar and sat on the stool next to Crowley. He had a drink in front of him.

"Hey, glad you could make it."

"Of course."

Another voice said, "What you gonna have?"

I looked up to see Hagen, my SeaBee builder, behind the bar wiping the space in front of me. We exchanged greetings and I ordered a Tom Collins. One of any drink that night would not have been enough and Hagen kept them coming as soon as we finished them. Actually when Crowley finished his drink, Hagen brought two more – one for each of us.

"You have to match me, you know."

No, I didn't know, but it was obvious it would be a cop out if I tried to do otherwise. I tried to order a Don Collins (just the non-alcoholic mix) but Hagen said that drink wasn't on the menu. So it stretched into a long evening. One or two of the men at the table passed us on the way to the restroom and stopped to talk to Crowley. Their stop always included a look at me, and Crowley always said, "This is Ensign Connolly – he's my director in the play." They would nod and say Hi, finish the chat and move on.

At about eleven o'clock there were still three or four Tom Collins sitting on the bar in front of me, undrunk, and without much prospect of being drunk.

"You got to finish, you know."

"Are you trying to get me drunk?"

"I wouldn't think of it."

I talked him into a truce: I would finish the ones staring at me, and he wouldn't order any more, or if he did, I didn't have to match them. It took a while, but eventually they were gone. Maybe Hagen decided to have mercy on me and made them very light. All the time Crowley was chattering about the Navy, the play, life after the Navy, going home, etc.

We walked slowly out of the club and into the warm night. The lighting was sufficient to show the white-painted stones along the walkway to the road. I was proud of myself meeting the challenge and being able to walk away; how far was uncertain. At the road we stopped; I thanked him for a "lovely evening" and we probably shook hands and laughed. He turned one way and headed into the dark toward the enlisted quarters. I turned the other; my pace to the Castle was slow and careful and my fall into bed was abrupt and careless. Sleep came quickly.

Chapter Sixteen

The Countdown:
To Be or Not to Be

2 December
Dear Folks –

News, news! I'm not long for Guam. At least not in the Rescue Center. The CG is giving up all Search and Rescue stations outside the U.S. except for Honolulu. That means all personnel attached to said stations will have to be reassigned. As yet I don't know where I'll be sent. Our orders haven't come in yet.

It is all happening very suddenly. Last week we got the official word. We are to be "decommissioned" by December 6. That means that the Navy will take over SAR on that date. We should be here a week or so longer in order to get things straightened out. There is a CG vessel waiting in the harbor on SAR duty. It will return to Honolulu instead of making the rest of its journey to Japan and Alaska. Some personnel and equipment might go back on it. Very probable. My action will depend upon my assignment. I could get assigned to one of the buoy tenders stationed on Guam or in the Philippines. If I get sent all the way to the states and be able to get home for Christmas, I'll let you know the soonest way possible.

There is only one bad thing about leaving. Our play comes off Dec 8 to 11. I hope we are still here. And I'd just as soon stay on Guam till after Christmas rather than be en route or in some strange place. But just about anyplace I go – Hono, S.F. or along the coast, I can find somebody to spend Christmas with. Two controllers are being discharged in S.F. around Feb. 1. Hope I get sent there again.

The stage is just about finished, and it is a beauty. I'm amazed that it turned out as well as it has. Of course, much is yet to be done. The front curtain to be rigged, drapes put up, the scenery painted, programs printed, etc. Even have to dig up a Christmas tree someplace. But the main work is through. We've been rehearsing on it for a week or so.

The completion of the stage is due to many hands. One commander who has a part in the play (Commander Barron – "Mr. Stanley") has practically turned his squadron into stagehands. He put two men to work on the stage instead of their regular duties. He's taken charge of the lighting, too, which is a big load off me. The Public Works department is painting the stage.

I told you that the NAS Commanding Officer, Captain Gazze, okayed a request for $51.98, and yet added a note that these funds be "carefully watched." Then he spent $100 for a couple of dinky signs on the station busses to support some football game. So far we have spent $18.75 and that on paint and make-up. However, lights may require the rest of the $50.00. I wrote to find out about royalty and found that $10 a performance is the charge for us out here. I have to ask for that amount yet, and probably I'll get it.

I'll be glad to get this play over with. And yet, now that I've got the stage to do with as I want, I hate to leave. I'd love to do "Mister Roberts, Glass Menagerie" and a couple of others. Well, that's the way the goose swings.

Love, Don

That was December 2nd, and we were scheduled to open on December 8th for four performances. December 11th would be the last.

It wasn't possible that Sarge and I would be shipped out before then, was it? Well, it was possible – decommissioning was December 6th – but it wasn't likely. Well, it was less likely than more likely because even though there was a Coast Guard ship in the harbor that would head to the states, and a Coast Guard plane would be arriving next week, there was paper work to be done and procedural stuff and the military never moves that fast! – do they?

And another thing! – we don't have our orders yet! – we don't know where we'll be going! Maybe "they" don't know either!

Everyone in the Rescue Center would be pulling up stakes, some with families, and going somewhere else, so there wasn't much benefit in mutual anguish or commiseration. No doubt Commander McCaffery tried to make some reassuring comments to me about not panicking; maybe the Little Theatre had become known as a Coast Guard project and it had to be carried to completion; maybe he could pull some strings and keep us around till the play was over. Of course, how good it would be, how worthwhile to "save" – that was always hovering overhead, at least over my head.

There was only one thing to do – keep the blue eyes focused straight ahead, not blink in the face of negative possibilities, follow the schedule and hope and pray for the best.

Moliere said that for "theatre," all you need is "a platform and a passion or two."   Less than a week before our opening, our "platform" was still in need of a few final elements, such as painted scenery.

By this time the production was close and I was going nuts. Rich Mueller, a St. Louis boy in VJ-1 squadron, made the frames for the scenery – the living room in the Stanley home – but he didn't get a chance to cover them, so Lloyd and I did that one afternoon. We finally got it painted – Sarge and I sprayed it. Of course, we needed a lot of props. Lucille Horton was in charge of props and before she dropped out got quite a bit. And we needed furniture, and not the rattan kind we have in the tropics. I went to Commander McDuffie and got to use some Public Works furniture in storage. It was maple.

Besides furniture a major set-piece was a Christmas tree that's on stage when the second act starts. It wasn't absolutely necessary for the plot – the characters wish each other Merry Christmas and gifts arrive to establish the season – but the tree, decorated and lighted, reinforced the contrast between the "peace" of the season and the chaos Whiteside was causing. There were scrub pine trees in the boondocks with long, saggy branches, but that was the best we could come up with. One was cut, put on a stand and decorated with lights and ornaments a day or so before opening night, to keep it fresh.

By opening night, December 8, we had a new stage with a nice set and adequate lighting.

The stage was ready to go.

Getting the actors to the same point was another story.

Not so much the characterizations or the stage movement or the memorizing, although all of those had their ups and downs. Basically, we had to be sure we had a full cast.

Miss Preen, the nurse, for example.

Tess Crider had dropped out to take care of kids with measles, and her husband wanted her to stay out.

For weeks I tried to get another Miss Preen, with no success. No one filled the bill. About three weeks before production Tess called me – she wanted to borrow a sailor uniform for a masquerade. I asked about the kids, who were well now, and then asked if she'd like to be in the play again. She was most anxious to, so she agreed to come to the next rehearsal. She showed up and then missed a couple. Then one night she called and told me she wouldn't be able to come – she and her husband had had a fight; at the time she was in the dispensary.

She missed a few rehearsals due to a black eye, but later came back. All her lines were memorized and she was good enough not to need all the remaining rehearsals.

She told me later that is was the first time he had hit her, but it was a good thing, because now she keeps her mouth shut. Some people are brutally frank.

Another missing character was Bert Jefferson. Omar's decision to give up the role was final; no cajoling could bring him back. It's hard now to imagine what my plan was if no Bert materialized with blocking and lines memorized; maybe I would play the part (I didn't want to – I'm too short to look good with Ann) and we could cut out the small role of the Professor that I was playing.

Well, one good thing led to another: Ann's husband Dick came back from Japan, which made Ann happy, and he agreed to play the part of Bert, which made me very happy. Dick was tall and lean, balding a bit, with a relaxed and friendly personality suitable for a small town newspaperman. He had about two weeks to learn the part and the blocking. But he was living with his stage partner and no doubt they rehearsed lines at home because he quickly learned his lines, developed his character and interacted nicely on stage.

I hoped Dick's return would allow Ann to relax and put more of herself into her character. In rehearsal her diction hadn't been very good. She was concerned about many other things and didn't focus on her role, so the character of Maggie, the brittle secretary, didn't have much force.

Her pregnancy was just beginning to show; her tall, slim build was working against us but she said she could dress to cover it up. Well, I thought, if her pregnancy does show, at least her "boy friend" is her husband.

There were a couple of parts that had a line or two – the neighbor women with small gifts and the radio technician setting up Whiteside's Christmas Eve broadcast. They were filled from the Navy support group. Four enlisted men played several walk-on roles – deliverymen, criminals, deputies, technicians – and four young girls were the Choir.

All told there were twenty-two adults and four children in the show. Many needed to learn the backstage protocols during a performance that put the right people in the right place at the right time. The walk-on actors served as the backstage crew with Castillo as stage manager; he had never done that before so that was another learning process. Backstage space was at a premium, for props and costumes, dressing "rooms" (an area on each side, a women's and a men's), and the lighting control board, not to mention space for the people who ran those things and actors ready to make their entrances.

As rehearsal progressed into the final weeks, it became obvious that we would be competing with other things besides the movies. A plane would warm up and it would be impossible to hear past the third row. A bus or man-haul would pass on the road, growling the whole time. But worst of all was the rain on the metal roof. The drumming of the rain would echo all over the Quonset, resembling a small boiler factory. This we could not control. I went to the security patrol and asked if they could slow down the busses, or rather, keep them from going into low gear when they passed the place. But the rain would come when it felt like it.

Three days before opening, we got word about our future – like a first shoe, just enough to tell us "what would happen;" the second shoe – "when" – was yet to come.

While we were rehearsing in the Armory that afternoon, the phone rang in the office at the end of the building. The yeoman came to the stage and looked up at us, so we stopped.

"Mrs. Yost?" he asked of everyone.

"Yes?"

"You got a phone call from your husband."

A phone call for a "theatre person" on an armory number probably hadn't happened before. It was a good idea, I felt, to keep out of the Navy's way as much as possible; our stage was enough of an intrusion. The call had to be important. There was no question Jan would take it.

Curious and concerned, she hurried off the stage and up the aisle. A few minutes later she sauntered back, beaming and bursting.

"Well," she said, "we know where we're going – to the Ironwood!"

That was the Coast Guard buoy tender stationed in Guam's Apra Harbor.

"Right here," she continued, "we staying right here!"

"Is that good?" I asked.

"Oh – that's what we wanted – so we can get our overseas time out of the way."

Military families share the life if not the duty, so "we" and "our" is normal speech about assignments.

"Oh – and Paul said you're going to St. Louis. Isn't that great?"

Wait. Me --to St. Louis?

St. Louis – "great"?

"That's your home, isn't it? Aren't you excited?"

I nodded a "yes." But – home? Really?

Everyone was excited for me.

I was stunned.

No doubt I was supposed to be happy; didn't everyone want to be close to home? My feeling was that I could always "go home" and there were so many other places that would be much more interesting. This was my chance to "see the world" and I was going home. I said I was glad, but –

We started rehearsing again, but Jan was so excited she couldn't concentrate and decided she might as well go home. The others stayed, so I had to play her part. It was one of her more flamboyant scenes and I tried to imitate her. Apparently I did a good job – we were all laughing and rehearsal wasn't very good.

The next night, two nights before opening, we had a "technical" rehearsal – we ran the show but the emphasis was on lighting and scene changes, the electronics and mechanics that need to work smoothly so the action continues as seamlessly as possible and the audience isn't aware of the changing.

There weren't any lighting changes during the play, within the acts, but we still had to be sure the lights worked properly. As for sound, there was no amplification – it was the "old days" of theatre when the actor's voice would have to reach the back of the theatre, as loud and clear as he/she wanted, without any sound system.

With lighting being tested, it was a chance to check makeup. Few of the actors had ever put on theatrical makeup, so those who had experience helped the others put on the right amount of rouge, helped them draw the fine dark lines under the eyes and put red dots at the corner of the eyes, next to the nose, to help the eyes stand out. That's what we did when I was acting in college and I passed it on to my actors.

There was only one set, the family living room, and changes such as the Christmas tree that was added for Act Two were minimal. But there were many props, and the backstage crew needed to rehearse getting them to the right people at the right time.

Unless actors understand the need to go through all of this so the technical crew can be sure of what they are doing, they get restless and frustrated because their performances are continually interrupted to make sure the technical elements are okay. And there was a final dress rehearsal – running the show straight through without any interruptions – awaiting them the next night.

My journal records that "I worked them like mad, so much that a few were beginning to get a little disgusted with it all – Lloyd especially." No doubt I had applied the ethic picked up in college that you don't have a good show if you don't work hard. Of course there's a balance – you can push too hard – but you give everything of yourself and hope that the others will follow.

If you have a bad dress rehearsal, the night before opening, with lots of problems, opening night will be good – that's the theatrical tradition. There's no record of whether ours was good or bad. No doubt it happened and went well enough. In any case, the next night we had to open.

All this was happening under the specter of Sarge and me being whisked off the island at a moment's notice. We had our orders and we knew our new assignments, but we didn't have a departure date. The decommissioning of the Rescue Center was December 6th, two days before opening night, and it was possible our departure would be expedited after that. No news was good news, but –

By opening night I had the usual combination of excitement and exhaustion, and no doubt, many of the others did, too. Everyone had worked hard – there's no better way to describe it – everyone wanted it to succeed. They knew what they had accomplished so far – a totally new stage in a place never likely to become a theatre, with a three-act Broadway play ready for presentation. Would anybody come? Would Guam Fever prevail or would possible patrons shake off routines and reach out to something new, something different? Would the nay-sayers triumph – "it can't be any good, don't waste your time." There was no time to think about that.

We gathered on the stage as I had done on every opening night in my experience. We held hands in unity, in encouragement – this was a group effort, we were a team and we had to pull together to bring this off. This production was a total "first" for this place. We had started from scratch – even lower than scratch – and now we had a good show. They could be proud of what they'd done.

That's about what I told them on opening night before the curtain went up.

And do your best, have fun, make it your own.

The Little Theatre
Naval Air Station, Agana
Presents

THE MAN WHO CAME
TO
DINNER

By George S. Kaufman
And Moss Hart

Directed
By
Donald Connolly

8, 9, 10, 11 December 1953   2000 Hours

Turn the cover and you read:

> "All the world's a stage," wrote Shakespeare. With the Little Theatre, however, it is just the opposite – this stage is all the world to us.
>
> When the idea of a little theatre on the station was first conceived, we realized that our first action would have to be the construction of a stage. With the permission and cooperation of Captain

Gazze and Lieutenant Commander Livingston, construction was begun in the Armory. Walter Hagen, BU2, is the man of "hammer and nails" whose know-how and will-do brought our idea to a reality. To him we are deeply grateful. We are also grateful to Lieutenant Commander K. C. McDuffie and Ensign Joseph Gulde for their generous assistance in its planning and construction.

Next came the lighting problem, and to handle this came Commander J. P. Barron and his squadron, VU-5. Their ability to make and borrow has furnished the stage with all its present lighting facilities. The curtains we owe to the resourcefulness of James Crowley, PR2, and R. C. Steketee, PR3. Again, a debt of gratitude to all.

And finally, to Captain O. P. Smoot, we express our thanks for that intangible but necessary ingredient, encouragement.

This production will be the first and, unfortunately, the last for some of us. We are confident, however, that this will be just the beginning of shows and entertainments on the station. No doubt much talent lies dormant among the several thousands hereabout; it is our hope that this stage and its facilities will aid in bringing them to the fore.

. . . . . .

As for the performances, I'll let the journal speak for what happened.

First, about the play. Have I mentioned that it was terrific? – much better than I had ever, ever hoped it would be. There wasn't a flaw in it, especially in the characters. It's amazing what amateurs can do; of course I worked them like mad, so much so that a few were beginning to be a little disgruntled with it all – Lloyd especially. But in the long run it was worth it, because even the smallest part came over perfectly and with good timing and interpretation.
No one was more surprised than I.
The first night's audience was small, disappointingly so. But it was a good audience, and the seventy-five people there made enough noise for a full house. Most of VU-5 came that night, and I can still hear Red Lucas laughing.
Lloyd came through fine, giving Whiteside just enough sarcasm. The real surprises were Ann Shay and Jewel Williams.

Since husband Dick had returned, Ann seemed a new person, more vital and focused. But in the final rehearsals she was focused on Dick, too – how he was doing. There was a lot for me to think about and most likely I didn't give Dick as much directorial attention as I should have. In my eyes, he was doing fine.

But on opening night she became the self-focused, brittle-but-longing woman that Whiteside had made her.

Ann stood straight and gave the lines all the force and variation they contained. Really fine. Got a lot of laughs. To hide the pregnancy she wore full skirts with large front pockets, or some sort of jacket, which worked.

Lloyd George (Sheridan Whiteside), Ann Shay (Maggie Cutler) and Don Connolly (Professor Metz) in *The Man Who Came to Dinner*

She need not have worried about Dick. He rolled through the part like a natural. For me it was the perfect ending to many fingers-crossed weeks.

As for Jewel Williams, by opening night she had somehow undergone a complete transformation. The "locked-up" lady of the rehearsals was living the part and "playing the audience" like a professional, milking every movement and every word for the appropriate laugh.

Jewel Williams as the idiot sister got a laugh on every entrance. She really floated; she'd stop on the stairs and look all around, then come down a few steps and say the first part of her line, then come down to Whiteside, and all in an old-womany way with an odd voice. And "floating."

Lloyd George (Sheridan Whiteside) and Jan Yost (Lorraine Sheldon) in *The Man Who Came to Dinner*

I really can't take credit for her perfection in the role. I might have planted the seeds, but she brought "Harriet" to full but understated bloom. It was marvelous to behold.

I haven't mentioned all the actors and extolled their performances. I wish I could recall some of each of them. There are bits that stand out – Jan Yost switching from fawning to flirting to anger to pathos when she discovers the plan to get rid of her; Dick Hollands as the British actor stuttering to imitate an English lord to lure her away; Jim Crowley as Banjo flicking his cigar and flickering his thick eyebrows as he closes Jan in the mummy case; Teresa Crider as Miss Preen walking

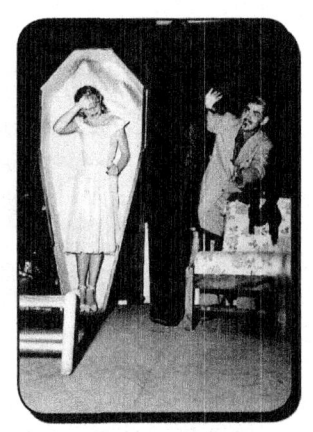

Jan Yost (Lorraine Sheldon) and Jim Crowley (Banjo) in *The Man Who Came to Dinner*

out on Whiteside with a speech that ends, "If Florence Nightingale had nursed you, Mr. Whiteside, she would have married Jack the Ripper instead of founding the Red Cross. Good day."

It was the play as I remembered it, as I remembered doing it – what can be called "actor-proof" because the characters, lines and situations are so good it would be hard to mess up and ruin the comedy. Maybe you could, but not with reasonable preparation and production.

Lieutenant Commander Livingston came opening night, said his wife made him. But he admitted he liked it: "I ain't had no college education or none a' that – you know what I mean? – but I thought it was pretty good." Then he said to Lloyd: "Hope it don't stop when Squirt here leaves."

Me –Squirt.

Teresa Crider's husband, Bob, came to see the show, and he was amazed, along with the rest of us. He came to the cast party, too, and as the story goes, all lived happily ever after – I hope.

The next morning at muster, Commander Tyrrel of Public Works gave a talk telling the men how good the play was; he and his wife came to see it again.

Sarge Horwood (Dr. Bradley) and Lloyd George (Sheridan Whiteside) in *The Man Who Came to Dinner*

There must have been a lot of word of mouth about the play because on the second night the Armory was almost full.

On the last two nights there was standing room only; in fact, people *were* standing down the sides.

Actors love nothing more than a responsive audience, and as the laughter came at the right places each night and seemed to roll on and on, they became more secure in their performances and played their roles with more assurance, handling their business more deftly and accommodating the variations that always occur in live performances. It was exciting to see all this unrolling, night after night.

As for the problems we anticipated, there were no revving planes and the busses and man-hauls managed to be fairly quiet as they passed. Maybe they were sent a different route; there was no mention of them at all.

But, as expected, we had rain.

Rain came when it felt like it; it had the feeling on the last three nights.

Tropical rain comes quite often in the late evening after the sun has gone down and the air cools a bit. The sky was clear every night when the show started. By the second act, clouds were passing overhead, and some time thereafter the rain fell.

The advance word to the actors about the rain was to stop the show if it fell too hard. But amateurs have a phobia about standing on stage doing nothing, or trying to adlib. So the first night of rain, they didn't stop, and it went okay. The second night of rain was worse: Banjo (Crowley) and Lloyd were on stage – it was the third act – and they kept right on going, even though I tried to stop them. So when Crowley walked off stage, I kept the next character from going on [I think I physically held him]. Lloyd finally got the idea and adlibbed something about "Terrible weather they have in Mesalia."

The third night of rain – the last performance – the rain started between the second and third acts. We held off starting the third act hoping it would stop, but it came only to a drizzle and stayed there. So we started, and were playing about five minutes when it really began to pour. Lloyd and Ann were in the middle of a big scene and they had to stop. Luckily they both kept character, with Lloyd adding a second comment about the weather to the one he had made the night before:

"Almost as bad as on Guam."

They waited a few seconds longer and the rain still kept up. Ann gave a sly smile and shook her finger at the roof. That brought down the house and everybody applauded. Shortly after that the rain stopped enough so we could continue, and we rang down the curtain to a full and satisfied house.

A special moment for me was at the beginning of the second act which takes place on Christmas Eve. The Christmas tree was in place in a prominent spot near the stairs in the rear. The tree lights were on and the stage lights were dim, and as the curtain rose and revealed the tree, there was a gasp of delight from the audience followed by applause. I think it said to the audience: this show is getting better all the time. That bit of extra work was worth it.

On the afternoon of December 9, the day after our opening, Sarge and I learned that a Coast Guard R5D plane was due on Saturday the 12th and wouldn't leave before Sunday, possibly Monday or Tuesday, returning to Honolulu.

We would be here for the rest of the show and maybe a few days after.

I probably yelled "Hallelujah." Sarge probably smiled and laughed a little. We could relax for the rest of the run.

Captain Gazze and his wife came on one of the later nights. Cushioned chairs were placed in the aisle at the back of the armory for them. They could have sat closer to the stage, but in the back they enjoyed the two electric fans mounted on the walls to blow directly on them. I never got any word whether or not they enjoyed it. Nor did I hear if Lieutenant Stegall, the new Special Services Officer, enjoyed it, or if he even attended.

After the last performance, Lloyd made a curtain speech. It was about me. He told the audience that I was being transferred and would be leaving the island in a few days, that I had been here four months, during which time I put on a few scenes in the "old" little theatre, and then had seen to the building of the "new" stage, and had directed this production. I was deeply touched. I realized that the big thing in my life while on Guam was the little theatre. Gad! But I wouldn't trade the experience for anything.

Curtain Call for the production of *The Man Who Came to Dinner*
NAS Agana, Guam, December 1953

Chapter Seventeen

Last Days

Those were busy days, that last week on Guam. I welcomed the end of them as anyone looks forward to a rest from labor and general weariness; yet, for fullness and enjoyment, they will be hard to equal. Those days gave me a funny combination of feelings: Physical weariness, from working on the play and being up late; anxiety, from the usual worries over all that could go wrong; satisfaction, after the huge success the show turned out to be; hustle and bustle, trying to get things ready to leave, whenever the word would come; worry, waiting for the word; and fun, at the beach in the afternoons and at the cast party Saturday night.

I must add one more – a tinge of sadness, as I waved to Lloyd through the plane window.

There must have been some sort of festivity after the performances, especially the last performance, at least for some of us – there had to be. There's no record of it in my journal. Maybe most of us were too weary and we decided that a good night's sleep on Friday would make a Saturday night cast party more enjoyable – and longer lasting.

The scheduled arrival of the Coast Guard plane on Saturday gave us 3 or 4 days, as far as we could figure, to get everything ready to go. Sarge and I did our washing at the Krechs who were now living in the Women Officers' Quarters while waiting for their house on the base. We had helped them move a week or so before, and had since enjoyed the view and breezes available in their living room. We also had some shopping to do – I was cursing myself for not having bought a suit or coat or something. It was going to be cold back home, and the cost much greater.

Then we received word that a typhoon was coming and our plane would be leaving early Sunday morning to avoid it. Our extra days on Guam had been wiped out.

During the day on Saturday a group of us took down the set and stored it, and cleaned out everything related to the play. So by Saturday night, we were both pretty tired, and packing and the cast party still lay ahead.

The party, which came first, was wonderful. It was held at Barron's house, roomy and well-furnished. I was so excited and in a whirl that I forgot that I told Donna who played the Stanley daughter I would see she got picked up. I used Sarge's car, and by the time I arrived at the party for the second time with Donna, the party was in full swing.

Everybody in the play was there. Joe Gulde was there – he had designed the stage and helped get wood for it; and Hagen, the SeaBee; and Rich Mueller, the guy from St. Louis who helped build the scenery, and Crowley, Castillo, French, Steketee and Thomas, and the Yosts, the Laings, Lloyd, Donna, the McDuffies, the Shays, Ann Scanland, the Criders, Barrons, Dick Dunkley (who was an extra), and Sarge and myself.

There was singing and dancing and drinking and eating; and the whole thing broke up around 3 a.m. We had a ham with a sign on it: "To Don Connely [their spelling!] the impresario – Bon Voyage and good hamming." Maggie McDuffie was responsible for the sentiment and spelling. Just before she left, Phyllis Laing gave me the Guamanian version of an Oscar – a small ivory statue of an oriental god of some sort. She read a little speech she had written.

It was all wonderful and ended much too soon. Sarge and I started packing about 3 a.m., and gave up and fell asleep at 5:00. At 6:00 we woke and finished packing, got everything on the plane and shortly after 7:00 we left. I woke up again near Wake Island.

Sarge and I must have been rarities (or oddities) on Guam those last few days. We wanted to stay a little longer so we could see what we had missed, and say sufficient good-byes to all the people we had met. It looked like another case of meet the people, get to know them, and then shove off for someplace else. We had been in the service just about a year, and we'd both been three or four places, as stations.

We said good-bye to the Krechs on Saturday afternoon, since we were going to different places that night, and we would be gone early Sunday morning. They gave us going-away-Christmas presents:

Sarge a wallet and me a pen and pencil set. And we had a farewell drink. It was typical of our whole relationship with them, this last meeting. The presents themselves were typical of their generosity and good-nature, and the plain, unpretentious manner of the whole occasion mirrored our evenings at bridge and at the Hospital club. Also the straight-forward departure with just the right amount of sentiment – all in good taste, and sincere. I think they were the hardest to leave.

The plane was leaving Sunday morning in order to avoid the typhoon heading toward the island, due in a day or so. We had seen one prolonged rain storm in our four months, but nothing that was really a typhoon; I rather wanted to have that "experience" but in the long run it wouldn't have been worth all the fuss.

At 7 a.m., we climbed aboard the plane and were just about seated when Lloyd climbed in. The propellers were starting to turn, and he was almost blown off the ladder; we talked for a couple of seconds, said good-bye again, and he climbed down. The plane taxied around, and he stood waving from the edge of the strip: that towering figure of unfettered dignity and good intention had gotten up after the long night, or had not gone to bed at all, in order to see us off. Knowing his love of sleep and his usual sleeping habits, I consider it a grand gesture.

I couldn't help think of the first night I saw him at the Officers Club, on Fight Night, when he was dancing a polka with somebody's wife, and Mosiman pointed him out from the bar – "That's Lloyd George. He's an Australian with an airline here. Quite a character." We had taught each other a lot on that little bit of land in the Pacific.

The sun was fully risen when we finally took off. A last glimpse showed the sunny, peaceful island it had been during most of our stay, but that soon disappeared in the distance, and in the mind, as sleep came. There was nothing in the heavens to tell of the storm that was approaching, that we were just missing by a matter of a day. We had arrived with the departure of one typhoon, and were leaving with the arrival of another. Perhaps we were blessed, or enchanted. In a way, the whole four months was blessed, and enchanted. I fear it will be once in a life time.

Chapter Eighteen

Goin' Home

(Time is slipping quickly by. Six months I have been in St. Louis, and in about nine more I'll be out of the Coast Guard. These months here in St. Louis have become very pleasant, but I'm certain that if I were to be here any longer, I'd put in for transfer.

(This journal was started at the suggestion of Galen Nielsen, the chief engineman I met at OCS and came to know in San Francisco when we met again in the personnel office in Alameda. There I made his friendship. That has been invaluable to me; they do not make a finer man.

(Galen suggested that I would like, someday, especially if I hope to do any writing, to be able to look back on these experiences; he said I'd forget them shortly if I didn't write them down. And he's right. Vivid experiences of a few months ago are fading. There are so many things I would like to put down, such as the return trip home, and the first months in service in San Francisco and Honolulu. So I'll take up where I left off – the trip home.)

Wake Island was about an hour away when I awoke. The Dramamine and general weariness from partying and packing had kept me in slumber the whole morning and part of the afternoon. We put down on Wake in time for chow, went to a movie at the base, and had a good sleep. The next night we were at Midway and managed to walk around a bit and eat some miserable chow.

It was chilly on Midway, different from when we went through in August. There was no swimming at all. People wore sweaters. There are a lot of fir trees on Midway, a lot of sand, and a lot of gooney birds. These are gull-like birds that look and act very stupidly. They walk off balance, can hardly fly, and do a mating dance that looks like first graders at a recital. Very colorful and good for laughs, which is good for Midway.

We just missed Russ French, our colleague in San Francisco, who had been a controller at Midway; he had left that afternoon, for the forward area, we thought. He had been assigned to one of the buoy boats on Guam. But we ran into him in Honolulu.

Honolulu lasted only two days for us; Sarge and I arrived on December 15th and departed on the morning of the 17th. The weather was wonderful – moderately warm during the day and just brisk at night, enough for a sweater or a sport coat. I vowed I'd have a suntan when I got home, so I spent one entire day on the beach at Ft. DeRussey where we stayed. I was a bit red and uncomfortable on the MATS plane to San Francisco, but tan I would be.

Getting that tan!

The Honolulu newspaper reported that a Navy plane from the Agana Air Station had been lost while on a Search and Rescue mission during the typhoon

I called Don Machado whom I had seen on the way out, and dropped into Rex Ravelle's body-building studio again. Our plane was preparing to leave on the 16th so we went to Hickam Field and waited. Bad weather in SanFran held us up until five the next morning. The plane was a Super-Constellation and the flight was terrific. Weather was still bad when we put down at Travis AFB, halfway to Sacramento. We waited for the bus to San Francisco until 7 p.m. and finally arrived there late that night.

It could have been the four months on Guam, which would make any stimulation of the senses through noise and activity seem pleasant. It could have been that this was the beginning of that magnificent illusion, "getting home." It could have been that it was just San Francisco. That is saying a lot.

I had not seen her in six months. In the absence I had idealized her very much; letters from people there had thrilled me. On my return she was still wonderful. She was alive, and warm, and at that moment very kind. I was very happy, having a kind of "returning hero" feeling, even though I was definitely no hero, and had not been gone long enough to really be returning. But SanFran looked great and was great; for once, I was happy to be swallowed by a crowd.

It was foggy. Most of the time there it was foggy. My Guam glands and corpuscles were forced to make a swift acclimation. A little too swift, it turned out, and a huge cold took hold of me for several days. I tried to sweat it out at the Marines Memorial where Sarge and I stayed, but to no avail. Eventually it went away.

My plans for getting home for Christmas were uncertain, hinging on whether Mom would be in St. Louis then. I called home and Mom said that she and Gram had been planning to go to Pontiac, Illinois, to visit Bob and Carol and the babies, but they wouldn't go now that I was coming home. So I made plane reservations for Christmas Eve, timing it to arrive in St. Louis about 10 p.m. that night. That gave me exactly one week in San Francisco.

Though the weather was not pleasant Sarge and I were in high spirits and were busy the whole week. The day of our arrival we had to check in at the base in Alameda where all the Coast Guard vessels tied up. It was there that I first saw Galen Nielsen when I reported to Commander, Western Area for RCC duty. Here again I ran into him, to the delight of us both.

I also ran into Mike McQueeny, the 83-boat skipper who became a friend that first time through; unfortunately his letter-writing habits had not kept the friendship alive. He was leaving for Seattle that night, with his fiancée, to spend the holidays with her folks. That was unfortunate – I would have liked to visit with them for a while.

We rented a car and first went to Ft. Point to see Brennan and the rest, the rest including Mr. Peterson, the skipper, who had changed his favorite swear word from "bullshit" to "horseshit." Brennan was much surprised; he hadn't expected us back so soon and had not expected us to bother to come to see him when we returned. Sarge is a great one for visiting friends he makes along the way; I'm glad some of that rubbed off on me.

Our return to the Rescue Center in the Appraisers Building was not anything special, even though our Frisco fiascoes had taken place there. Lieutenant Commander Shannon and Chief Dygert were there;

Weber was gone, as were Morgan and Bauman, the quartermasters, and Garrigues, the aerographer. It wasn't the old place and we didn't stay very long.

The Nielsens – Galen, Louise, and Carole – Christmas 1953

I saw the Neilsens several times; they were as wonderful and likeable and unassuming as ever. Their kindness to me when I arrived in April, their friendship in the few months there, and their farewell at Alameda when I left for Honolulu are bright spots in my recollections of San Francisco. There were the "Krechs" of San Francisco.

There was no opportunity for picnics at the beach or shows with them. We just sat and talked. I helped Galen write a letter asking for release from the Coast Guard. He's been a chief for four of the eight years he's been in the service; now that a commission has been denied him, he sees no future in staying in. I agree, and did all I could to help.

Then there were the Stephens, from Hillsborough, with the swimming pool in the back yard. I had been there several times, and upon return, gave them a ring.

Mrs. Stephens said she had tried to find my Guam address to thank me for the jellies from Honolulu. She had called some Coast Guard offices in San Francisco but they couldn't provide it. So she was happy when I called.

Sarge and I were invited for dinner, but not at their home. They took us to an elegant restaurant in San Mateo. It was a pleasant evening with drinks at their home first, and dinner, and conversation to match the surroundings, like curtains.

I went to see "New Faces of 1952," a show I had first heard about in OCS when somebody brought the records and we played them in moments of relaxation. On Guam I bought my own set and played them as often as I could – not very much. So an opportunity to see the show struck me as wonderful. And my hopes were not disappointed. The show was sparkling, alive, funny, sentimental, and completely entertaining. All this, even though I had practically memorized the lyrics. The people in the audience were alive, too, and showed their appreciation of the clever touches as well as the broad. My own appreciation must have been very apparent. At the end of the show, a middle-aged lady in back of me said, "Have you seen the show before?" "No," I replied, "why do you ask?" "Well," she said, "we enjoyed your enthusiasm so much, we thought you must have seen it before."

I visited Sister Jane Francis Connolly in Oakland one afternoon; she hoped I would stay over Christmas and would come to Oakland for Christmas Day. Everyone extended invitations for Christmas dinner IF I was going to be around.

Sarge's assignment was in San Francisco; I secretly envied him. If I had made such a statement out loud, most people would have thought I was crazy. My envy was not particularly apparent that week because the idea of "Home for Christmas" and the general holiday atmosphere and the simple fact of being back in the states kept me occupied. I bought a new suit and a sweater, and sent Christmas cards to the people still on Guam. This last was an awakener: just three weeks before I had sent cards from Guam to the people in the states, and now, still before Christmas, I was doing the reverse.

On December 24, 1953, I left San Francisco for the second time, heading east to the old environs. All in all, I was looking forward to getting home and at the same time was sorry to leave. The holiday spirit carried me over the hump with a minimum of nostalgia.

The plane landed at the St. Louis airport at approximately 10 p.m. Christmas Eve – finally home – 7,000 miles: all this was going through my mind while leaving the plane. Who would I see? How much would they, and familiar places, have changed? The wind was blowing steadily, but it was not very cold and there was no snow on the ground. The temperature was crisp and exhilarating, in keeping with the mood.

My welcoming committee consisted of Tom Hertich, a boyhood friend and neighbor. He explained that Mom and Gram had gone to Illinois anyway, because Gram was so set on going, and Mom hated to disappoint her. We went home, where Jim was dressing to take a date to Midnight Mass. I washed and shaved and changed clothes, and Tom and I went to Midnight Mass at St. Ann's.

Looking back, I wonder if the fact that it was Christmas made this abortive homecoming easier to take. It seems like it would have made it harder. But I was determined to enjoy it, and in the long run did so.

After Mass the whole Normandy gang had breakfast at the Wyers' house. Just about everybody was there except Gracie and Angelo who were at home with their new baby. I had been the only one missing, and with my countenance brightly displayed above a bright red shirt recently purchased, the circle was complete. The breakfast was terrific and lasted until 4 a.m. or so, with everyone in good spirits. As I poured coffee, I was greeted with calls of "mess boy!"

Then in the next few days the gang called at various homes and visited, just like we did during high school and college. I went to Gracie's grandmother's house for Christmas dinner.

While Mom was gone I got a lot of preliminary calls and visits out of the way. There was a certain sadistic pleasure in calling up a friend, talking for a few moments, and finally surprising the hell out of them. "What are you doing here?" was the inevitable question. My reply, "I'm being stationed here" caused even more surprise.

My "proceed and travel time" expired on 31 December 1953. About 7:30 that evening I called the Coast Guard office; the next working day was January 4. I wound up with three extra days.

My order assigned me to the Reserve Office, as Assistant Director. My knowledge of reserve matters was absolutely nil; however, I had been in the service long enough to realize that in most cases, nothing was too difficult to pick up. Or if it did prove difficult, there was always somebody else to refer to.

On the first duty day, waiting on the street corner for the bus that morning, I was asked by a man, "You reporting for duty?" It turned out he was a Lieutenant Commander in charge of Coast Guard personnel. So early on the first day, even before reporting in, I was being indoctrinated.

Together we walked into Second Coast Guard District Headquarters in downtown St. Louis where my sojourn in the military and the world beyond enclosures had begun.
The name of the officer I was with was John L. Barron.
St. Louis – again?
Another John Barron?
Was my Guam adventure going to repeat itself?
No. No, not possible.

Chapter Nineteen

And Then –

My active duty in the Coast Guard ended on December 1, 1954, almost exactly two years after I had been sworn in. The expected time had been shortened by four months – the period spent at OCS; originally those months weren't to be counted toward our two year obligation, but with the war ended Reservists were being released as soon as possible, even those with active duty time from World War II who had been recalled for the Korean War.

That was it for me. No more Coast Guard, no more Reserve or military connection of any kind for me. I could see no reason to think about anything but landing a job and getting started on a career.

I also said the same thing about more higher education. Four years were enough.

After one year working at a television station in Quincy, Illinois, writing and producing commercials, both those attitudes were reversed. With television plays becoming an every-night affair and very popular, spawning writers like Paddy Chayefsky, Rod Serling and Horton Foote, I decided to enter a graduate program (thanks to the G.I. Bill) at the University of Southern California in Los Angeles, the city where most of the plays were being produced.

Once in Los Angeles, knowing no one except a few relatives and family friends, I realized that attending some reserve drills would be a way to meet people and make extra money. After a few months probation, the 11th District Reserve Office accepted me and assigned me to the Tuesday night unit at the Training Center at Chavez Ravine (now the site of Dodger Stadium).

Two years later when, master's degree in hand, I took a job in Bethesda, Maryland, I decided to continue the Reserve connection for the same reasons. When Barbara and I married there in 1961, she was a nurse in the Navy and appreciated the military connection. It continued, one night a week, or one weekend a month, plus two weeks training until 1975, when I retired as a Commander.

Today we still enjoy the benefits.

In my journal I said I might buy a bicycle on Guam, and that I wanted to go to school in Europe. I didn't do either. And that last lesson in my USAFI course in German?—I never finished it.

That's me, and today is a long time from the 1953 world of this Blue-Eyed Ensign. Telling that story has brought those people and events alive to me, especially with the letters and journal that caught them at the time.

Some of the people stayed in my life for a long time, some a short time, some not at all. And some popped up once to the surprise of both parties.

Of the Coast Guard people:

Galen Nielsen and his wife Louise became close friends with me and my wife. Galen served twenty years in the Coast Guard, became a Chief Warrant Officer, and by the time of his retirement had achieved the rank of Lieutenant. His entire career was on the west coast and Alaska except for some training programs in Virginia, which allowed him to visit me and meet Barbara.

He was with Barbara and me the weekend we got engaged, helping us through some tentative early moments. After he retired and their four daughters were on their own, he and Louise worked many years for companies in the Middle East. A widower, he lives in the west but still travels, so we see him occasionally. He sends my wife flowers at Christmas.

Sarge Horwood married and went to medical school. He and his wife Carla received medical degrees together from Case Western Reserve University. Barb and I visited them in Cleveland when each couple had small children, and they returned the visit to us in Bethesda. Letters and Christmas cards followed for a while.

Sometime later there was another marriage, and after a move to Canada, we lost touch. Sarge is listed as author and co-author of articles in *Pediatrics* and other medical journals.

When Paul Yost served as Commandant of the Coast Guard from 1986 to 1990 (the highest position in the service), he and Jan lived in the Commandant's residence in Kenwood, only a few miles from our home. I was tempted to make contact then, but never followed through.

About ten years ago I spotted them in the lobby of a local movie theatre. It was a rushed meeting and I'm not sure they realized who I was.

In the last weeks of writing this, I felt I should try to contact them at least to verify some Coast Guard information, so I googled them and found an address nearby and a phone number. Also a recent photo of them. I called and left a message.

The next day, December 4, 2014, I was playing doubles tennis at the local Tennis Center, as I had been every Thursday since September, when the foursome arrived on the court next to ours, at their regular Thursday time. I had noticed the group and realized that two of them who usually arrived early were a couple.

On this day, after about 20 minutes of playing, I happened to be facing toward them and the photo popped into my head. After staring at them for a few seconds, I gasped, "Oh my God." To the bewilderment of my group, I left our game and hurried to the netting separating the courts and called, "Paul?" The man looked up. I repeated, "Paul?" He replied, "Yes – Paul Yost." I called "Jan!" and they came toward the netting, themselves bewildered. "I served with you on Guam!" After brief exchanges we went back to our games, and afterward we visited for half-an-hour. I told them about the book and we exchanged phone numbers.

Lee Harrison III followed his artistic bent and is considered a pioneer in analog computer animation. In the late 1950s he earned an engineering degree from Washington University in St. Louis. In 1969 he founded the Computer Image Corporation in Denver, Colorado where he lived until his death in 1998. By accident or design, he called on me when I was a principal in a small film company, Charlie-Papa Productions in Rockville, Maryland in the 1970s. We were too small to be able to be involved in his work and the connection was never pursued. He is best known as the inventor of Scanimate and the ANIMAC. He received an Emmy Award in 1972 for his work.

Mike McQueeny settled in his hometown of Kansas City, Missouri, where I visited him once when driving from California home to St. Louis. He stayed in the Coast Guard Reserve; his death was listed in the publication for CG retirees.

Of the Navy people, the most memorable and long lasting are Shep and Nora Krech.

My move to Bethesda in 1958 put me a two-hour drive from their new home on the other side of the Chesapeake Bay and I visited often. I was working in medical television at the National Naval Medical Center, and Nora was concerned that commercial television would be a menace to their lifestyle and didn't want one of those clunky sets in her house or an antenna on the roof. To watch one of the Nixon-Kennedy debates in 1960 at their home, I brought my portable black-and-white set, the size of a suitcase, with rabbit-ears for an antenna. This, she realized, she could put in a closet, so it was acceptable.

They hosted my mother and brother, Father Luke, when those two came to visit me, and Barbara when we started dating. They helped me plan my first trip to Europe in 1960, providing suggestions of places to go and people to contact.

Barbara and I became engaged in December 1960 and in February we were invited for a winter weekend. Appropriately Nora wrote an individual invitation to Barbara. The weekend was memorable because a heavy snow storm was passing through which made driving difficult, even in my new Volkswagen Beetle I had bought in Europe. When we arrived at the road leading to their house, a small tractor was waiting to drag the car across the deep snow to the house. The two days were spent in conversation, bridge playing, drinking and dining, usually close to a crackling fireplace.

They came to our wedding in April 1961.

There were fewer visits as our children came and grew and theirs finished school and married and grandchildren came along. Shep continued his general medical practice and served as head of the county school board. The written word still appealed to Nora: After receiving my Christmas letter one year – I try to make them entertaining as well as newsy – Nora telephoned to express her enjoyment.

In their later years they sold their house and built a smaller, one-story place on a part of the property. As Nora developed Alzheimer's disease, we didn't see her again. Several times we picked up Shep at the new house and took him to a seafood lunch, complete with a martini.

Nora was almost 90 years old when she died in 2006. Shep died 15 months later at age 88.

Of the Navy/Theatre people, Jim Crowley stands out. He returned to Keansburg, New Jersey and after a few years married Patricia. He and I corresponded, which included an invitation to my wedding. He and Pat came, and it was a nostalgic reunion. We continued exchanging Christmas cards for a while. In a phone conversation with Patricia in October 2014, I learned that Jim died six years before. They have six children. Their son served a tour in the Coast Guard, and a grandson is a graduate of the Coast Guard Academy who hopes to make a career of the service.

Ann and Dick Shay stayed in touch for a few years primarily via Christmas cards. Dick was stationed at Sandia base in New Mexico when I was driving to graduate school in Los Angeles in 1956, and I stopped to see them and was able to see the little one who had been on stage in secret with his/her mother.

I probably informed them when I was getting married; Ann was always interested in my love life.

My meeting with Rinald Steketee ("Stek") confounded both of us. He was a supervisor at a Postal Service facility in Tacoma, Washington, and in the late 1980s I was there on a filming assignment. I recognized his last name on his identification tag, and asked if he had a brother who had been in the navy on Guam. When he said he had been there, I did a double take and started explaining who I was. He remembered the play, but he couldn't connect the guy talking to him with the ensign who had directed the play. At dinner in the cafeteria we sorted it out.

Finally there is Lloyd George.

Lloyd stayed on Guam long enough to take over the Little Theatre and produce and act in another play in "our" theatre, "The Male Animal." He was proud of his accomplishment and so was I, although this time I questioned his choice as being too sophisticated.

His employer, Qantas, moved him to Kuala Lumpur, Malaysia, and then to Athens. We corresponded with reasonable frequency, sharing the vagaries of our situations. He was especially pleased to be in Athens and participate in European culture.

By the autumn of 1960 there had been no correspondence for a while. My vacation in Europe that year didn't include Athens, but it was possible that he might have been transferred to London or Copenhagen or Rome or Paris, where I was going to visit.

In London, the first stop on my trip, my goal was to see as many plays as possible in a five-day stay. I would visit the historical places and museums early in the day, and have the rest of the day for theatre, sometimes seeing two shows a day. Leaving a theatre late on a dark rainy afternoon and looking for a place for a meal before the evening show, I saw the name "QANTAS, a neon sign piercing the mist at the front of a ticket office.

Maybe they could tell me where Lloyd was.

The manager nodded when I mentioned Lloyd's name and listened passively as I explained how I knew him, that we had been corresponding but not lately, and I hoped maybe he might be some place I was going to be. The embellished explanation seemed necessary so the manager wouldn't think there was nefarious reason for my search – cold war intrigue was prominent at the time.

At the end of my prolonged recitation, the manager said, "I'm sorry to tell you, your friend has died."

What?

My friend has died? What?!

Impossible! I mean –

When I knew him, he was fine –

The manager added, "Yes, he had a heart attack."

He was so young –

I can't believe it –

I stammered all of those and more, breathlessly spilling little bits about Lloyd that would display our connection and maybe, somehow, prove he couldn't be dead.

But he was.

The manager continued to listen respectfully, without a change in expression.

Finally I said, "Thank you" and leaned into the door that let me out into the misty darkness. There was some comfort in the envelop it put around me. In the wet, reddish glow of the Qantas sign, awash in thoughts of that man so tied to my life on that faraway island, my body shook, my blue eyes dimmed, filled, and spilled over.